AD Architectural Design

Space Architecture

Guest-edited by Rachel Armstrong

WILEY-ACADEMY

Architectural Design
Vol 70 No 2 March 2000

ISBN 0-471-86438-2
Profile No 144

Editorial Offices
International House
Ealing Broadway Centre
London W5 5DB
T: +44 (0)20 8326 3800
F: +44 (0)20 8326 3801
E: info@wiley.co.uk

Editor
Maggie Toy

Guest Editor
Dr Rachel Armstrong

Managing Editor
Helen Castle

Production
Mariangela Palazzi-Williams

Art Director
Christian Küsters

Design Assistant
Owen Peyton Jones

Advertisement Sales
01243 843272

Editorial Board
Denise Bratton
Peter Cook
Massimiliano Fuksas
Charles Jencks
Jan Kaplicky
Robert Maxwell
Jayne Merkel
Monica Pidgeon
Antoine Predock
Leon van Schaik

Photo Credits
ᴭ Architectural Design

Abbreviated positions
b=bottom, c=centre, l=left, r=right, t=top

p 6 and 8(t) Courtesy Leo A Daly, photos © Paul Brokering; p 7 photo courtesy San Diego Aerospace Museum Archives; p 8(b) photo courtesy Boeing Historical Archives; p 9(t) photo courtesy John Frassanito & Associates; p 9(b) STAR TREKTM and © 1998 Paramount Pictures Corporation, All Rights Reserved, photo courtesy of the Landmark Entertainment Group; pp 11–15 and 17 drawings courtesy of David Ashford; p 18 courtesy WildWings; p 22(l) courtesy Japanese Rocket Society (JRS); pp 21, 22 (r) and 23 courtesy Shimizu Corporation; pp 24–25 courtesy Wimberly Allison Tong & Goo; p 26 courtesy American Museum of Natural History, © R Williams (STScI), NASA; pp 27–29 © D Finnin / American Museum of Natural History; p 30 photos © Thomas Taylor; p 35 courtesy X-PRIZE Foundation; p 37 courtesy Jason Skeet of the AAA, © AAA; pp 40-43 courtesy Suzanne Lee, © SPORE; p 44 © Simon Thorogood; pp 48-59 all images courtesy Ted Krueger, © School of Architecture, University of Arkansas, with the exception of p53(bl) and 58(br) courtesy Ted Krueger, © NASA; pp 60-61 paintings © Robert T McCall; pp 62-65 all images © Mathis Osterhage; pp 66-70 all images © Esther De Angelis; pp 80 and 81 © Branson Coates Architecture, photos: Graham Gaunt;

p 82 courtesy Marc Newson Architect, © IDEE Company, Japan; p 83 courtesy Misha Stefan, photo: Kate Martin; pp 84 and 85 courtesy the Rachel Rosenthal Company, photo © Annie Leibovitz; pp 86 and 88–89 © Peter Cook.

ᴭ Plus
pp 94–95 courtesy Mark Fisher; p 96 © Nicky J Sims/Redferns; p 97 courtesy Zaha Hadid, photo: Oliver Domeisen; p 98 cover photo: © Monica Pidgeon; pp 100-101 all cover photos: © Monica Pidgeon; p 102 (t) courtesy Clare Design, portrait photo: Peter Hyatt; pp 102 and 104 photos of Clare Residence courtesy Clare Design, by Adrian Boddy, Richard Stringer and Lindy Atkin; p 105–108 courtesy Clare Design; p 112 *The Kitchen* from 'A Home' series, c 1865 (w/c on paper) by Carl Larsson (1853–1919) Nationalmuseum, Stockholm, Sweden/Bridgeman Art Library.

The Site Lines article on p 112 was the result of research that Wendy Hitchmough carried out as a Churchill Fellow to Sweden: Winston Churchill Memorial Trust (www.wcmt.org.uk).

Subscription Offices UK
John Wiley & Sons Ltd.
Journals Administration Department
1 Oaklands Way, Bognor Regis
West Sussex, PO22 9SA
T: +44 (0)1243 843272
F: +44 (0)1243 843232
E: cs-journals@wiley.co.uk

Subscription Offices USA and Canada
John Wiley & Sons Ltd.
Journals Administration Department
605 Third Avenue
New York, NY 10158
T: +1 212 850 6645
F: +1 212 850 6021
E: subinfo@wiley.com

Annual Subscription Rates 2000
Institutional Rate: UK £135
Personal Rate: UK £90
OUTSIDE UK
Institutional Rate: US $225
Personal Rate: US $105

ᴭ is published bi-monthly.
Prices are for six issues and include postage and handling charges. Periodicals postage paid at Jamaica, NY 11431. Air freight and mailing in the USA by Publications Expediting Services Inc, 200 Meacham Avenue, Elmont, NY 11003

Single Issues UK: £19.99
Single Issues outside UK: US $32.50
Order two or more titles and postage is free. For orders of one title ad £2.00/US $5.00. To receive order by air please add £5.50/US $10.00

Postmaster
Send address changes to ᴭ c/o Expediting Services Inc, 200 Meacham Avenue, Elmont, NY 11003

Printed in Italy. All prices are subject to change without notice.
[ISSN: 0003-8504]

Space Architecture
Guest Editor Rachel Armstrong

∆D Architectural Design +

This millennium space issue of *Architectural Design* could not be more timely. In February 1967, △ published a special issue of the magazine entitled *2000+*. Guest-edited by John McHale – then Executive Director and Research Associate of the World Resources Inventory at Southern Illinois – it largely focused on the technological aspects of space, including lots of black and white photos of space vehicles, rockets and astronauts. McHale, who Kenneth Frampton describes in his *Modern Architecture: A Critical History* (Thames and Hudson, 1992) as a British apologist for Buckminster Fuller, regarded the 'imagery' of technology in itself as a powerful agency of change for architecture, which was then largely 'hidebound by a vision of the fine arts'.

Though the high-tech imagery of space still has the same appeal for architects today as it did to McHale and the staff of △ 33 years ago, we have chosen in this issue not to concentrate on the surface appearance of space equipment and vehicles. Instead the publication challenges architects to design for space. In accordance with this, it is guest-edited by Dr Rachel Armstrong, a tutor at the Bartlett School of Architecture in London, who has a unique background as a medical doctor, which she uses to teach her architectural students about the body. Armstrong was first engaged by the subject of space when she realised the physical connotations of designing for environments with no gravity; in space, humans become totally dependent on their surrounding architecture or vehicular environments, in a way that they are not on Earth.

Space Architecture heralds an entirely new era of space exploration and development, in which architects must take their place. Unlike the Cold War era of space-related design, which John Zukowsky, Curator of Architecture at the Art Institute of Chicago, describes in his opening essay as being dominated by government agencies, space is now being opened up for public access by private enterprise and individuals. The issue illustrates projects by some pioneering entrepreneurial companies, such as WAT&G, Shimizu Systems and the X-Prize Contenders. The prospect of a substantial space tourism industry is endorsed through contributions from a wide range of specialists. They include the engineer David Ashford, Director of Bristol Spaceplanes Limited, and the economist Patrick Collins, Vice President of Spacetopia and Guest Researcher at NASDA (the Japanese Space Agency), who describe the viability of such an industry in terms of vehicle development and economic feasibility. It is inevitable that the reality of designing for space – the most extreme of environments, without gravity, and with few structural prototypes – will radically change architectural processes. Some insight into how architectural practice might evolve is given by Ted Krueger, Director of Information Technology at the School of Architecture, University of Arkansas, who organised a design studio with David Fitts, an architect with the flight crew support group at NASA.

With most specialists in the field predicting that relaunchable space planes will be making regular chartered flights into space by the year 2020, the extent to which the extraterrestial will have been opened up as an alternative inhabitable environment in a further 30 years can only be guessed at. *Maggie Toy*

A template for the future city has been carved into the heavens. Ever since the beginning of humankind, we have looked to the sky for the opportunity to make a new start in our imperfect world. Between the stars and the darkness we have imagined utopias beyond the reach of our travel technologies, colonising space with our fantasies.

Until the 20th century, leaving the Earth's surface remained a fantasy. But with the advent of the space race and the first ventures into orbit in the middle of this era, this changed forever. Yet, despite the initial success and the resulting enthusiasm for space projects, few people are aware that space travel for ordinary people is imminent, and even when presented with the arguments, many seem unable to accept the idea.

This reluctance to believe in extra-terrestrial living can be seen as a significant failing in modern society. It suggests disillusionment and lack of conviction about the successful future of humankind. Yet it is important for a society to have ambitions for the future. The conquering of space is a unique challenge that can help to unify the world and encourage us to collaborate as a species. In the emerging global society, this collective project is essential not just as a symbol of human unity, but for future economic progress. After all, the story of the human race through exploration and expansion into new territories and environments, and the eventual establishment of cities, is the essence of civilisation.

Although the Apollo 11 Moon landings took place just over 30 years ago, when serious study began on the establishment of human colonies on other planets, space beyond the limits of terrestrial gravity is still considered a mystery belonging to the realms of science fiction. In his landmark publication *The High Frontier*, Gerard K O'Neill confidently predicted that 'construction of a high orbital facility could begin within seven to ten years on the basis of technology now being developed for the space-shuttle and it could be completed within 15 to 25 years'.[1] This promise has not yet been delivered.

In February 1967, *D* published a space issue looking at the projects and technologies that would draw architects' attention towards extra-terrestrial projects, and it is surprising how current the contributors' views remain.[2] What has changed recently is that the largest industry in the world – tourism – is being tapped as the source of vision and funding to open

space up to the general public. The feasibility of this idea was confirmed by NASA in 1998.[3]

Consequently, when putting this special issue together, my aim was to bring readers up to date on how much progress has been made towards establishing a civilian presence in orbit, and to illustrate the range of real projects now pending. I have selected a diverse range of authors from the aerospace industry, architecture, contemporary culture and the leisure industry to illustrate the wide-ranging influence that orbital projects will have on our lives in the near future as popular tourist destinations. It is impossible to ignore the environmental impact that a booming industry in space travel will have on the Earth, and this issue is addressed by an equally varied selection of experts. Cultural activists, scientists and social commentators examine how we will achieve our desire to venture into a relatively unexplored habitat, what the risks and benefits are and how settlement will eventually transform the surface of other planets to support human life.

Perhaps the most intriguing aspect of space habitation will be its effects on the human body. Those who actually live in space will become completely dependent for their survival on the technology and architecture inside which they live. This will pose moral and ethical dilemmas for the budding commercial space industry, since the facilities, architectural surroundings and even the clothes used in outer space will place selective pressures on the human body. Taken to its extreme conclusion, this will mean that space-dwelling humans will gradually adapt and evolve to embrace a life style that is completely dependent on machines. In this 'life and death' environment, there may ultimately be no choice about whether to hybridise our bodies with synthetic inventions or genetic upgrading, since the imperative will be survival.

Architects of these new habitats will need to reflect on the comfort, health and survival of their occupants. Such speculation on the direct link between the body and its architectural surroundings may inspire traditional architects to think the unthinkable, becoming involved in the design of the current embryonic projects. It is to be hoped that in the near future, architects and students may discard their terrestrial prejudices, leave behind the conventions of gravity and join the engineers, designers and citizens who are working to realise the first determined attempts to live beyond Earth. *D*

Dr Rachel Armstrong

Notes
1 Gerard K O'Neill, *The High Frontier: Human Colonies In Space*, Corgi (London), 1978.
2 *Architectural Digest*, London, February 1967.
3 'General Public Space Travel and Tourism', NASA/STA joint study, NP-1998-03-11-MSFC, March 1998.

Architects in Space

By way of introduction to the subject of space architecture, John Zukowsky, the Curator of Architecture at the Art Institute of Chicago, considers the contribution that architects have already made in the development of space-related structures. Tracing the association between outer orbits and the stars as far back as the design of observatories in the 17th century, he concentrates on the technological and explorational leaps of the postwar years.

Architects in space! Yes, that's where some clients and critics would like to see many of them – sent to the Moon and beyond in order to free Earth of their design excesses. Yet there is a more serious side to the idea. Architects have often been actively involved in designing for space – an example is Paolo Soleri, who proposed space environments and space homes – or for science-fiction projects, like some of the sets for *Star Trek* designed by Frank Israel. Mostly, however, the work that architects have conceived for space exploration has related to the nuts and bolts of military and political use of space, particularly as regards the post-World War II era of the Cold War.

An exhibition entitled *2001. Building for Space Travel* is scheduled to take place in 2001–02 at the Art Institute of Chicago and the Museum of Flight in Seattle. This project and the accompanying book will explore the role that architects, industrial designers and graphic designers – visual arts professionals as opposed to scientists or aerospace engineers – have played in shaping architecture and design for space travel. In some ways, it constitutes a sequel to the Art Institute's successful 1996 book and exhibition, *Building for Air Travel. Architecture and Design for Commercial Aviation*. That project examined the impact that architects and designers have had on air travel since the end of World War I, from airports and aircraft factories to aeroplane interiors and airline corporate identity. With a background spanning more than seven decades of building for the aerospace industry, is it any surprise that architects have made a substantial contribution to space exploration?

Although architects have designed space-related buildings such as observatories since the 16th and 17th centuries – these include Sir Christopher Wren's Royal Observatory at Greenwich (1675) – their earliest contributions to designing space facilities as we know them – launch pads and gantries – date back to the first real spaceship of the 20th century. This was the V-2 or A-4 ballistic missile, developed by the German army during World War II. It was first launched successfully on 3 October 1942, when the head of its development programme, General Walter Dornberger, proclaimed, 'Today the space ship is born!' Indeed, V-2s reached speeds of about 3,500 miles per hour and altitudes of 55 miles, approaching the edge of the atmosphere. German architects who worked for the Luftwaffe – the Deutsche Arbeitsfront (German Labour Organisation) and Baugruppe

Schlempp, headed by architect Walther Schlempp – designed and created the assembly, launch and testing facilities at Peenemuende. These were later extensively damaged in the British and American bombing raids of 17–18 August 1943 and summer 1944. With the end of World War II, this German wonder-weapon became, in part, the basis of Allied rocket programmes in the United States, Britain, France and the Soviet Union.

In our minds, the nuclear missile race and related space race between the United States and the Soviet Union are as much a part of the Cold War as events like the Berlin Airlift of 1948. Structures such as the FBI Building in Washington by CF Murphy Associates (1963–75), complexes for the CIA, MI5 and the KGB, or the more powerfully expressive yet sinister Berlin Wall and the 'Sputnik-like' broadcasting tower in East Berlin from the 1960s, can be seen as the monuments of those years of confrontation between East and West. Architects during the Cold War also designed missile-assembly and launch facilities. In the United States, these range from the work done by DMJM (Daniel Mann Johnson & Mendenhall), the Parsons Group and Sverdrup on underground silos and mobile train launchers for intercontinental ballistic missiles (ICBMS), to enormous industrial complexes for creating these missiles, the most famous of which is the showpiece Convair factory (1955–57), outside San Diego, by Charles Luckman and William Pereira. Constructed to build the Atlas missile, America's first ICBM, it housed 12,000 employees.

Beyond the military-related work carried out by architects in the Cold War, arguably the most impressive space-race facilities in the USA are those at Cape Canaveral's Kennedy Space Center, built in 1962 by a consortium called URSAM, led by architect Max O Urbahn from New York. With Anton Tedesko of Roberts and Schaefer as the engineering consultant, Urbahn designed the vertical assembly building (VAB) to house four of Wernher von Braun's massive Saturn launchers, each more than 30 storeys high. It was here that they were mated with Apollo capsules before being transported vertically to the launch pads via an

enormous tractor called the crawler. The launch-control complex designed by Urbahn featured pivoting panels that would protect its angled glass walls from vibrations during launches. When these facilities were first designed and constructed, they received extensive coverage in architectural journals such as *Architectural Forum* (September 1963 and January–February 1967), *Progressive Architecture* (March 1965) and *L'Architecture d'Aujourd'hui* (September 1967). They were even included in the New York Museum of Modern Art's 1964 exhibition, *Twentieth Century Engineering*. The Kennedy Space Center facilities, altered by other architects, are still in use today for the space shuttle launches. They are a monument to President Kennedy's famous speech of 1961, in which he stated the determination of the United States to reach the Moon within that decade – a feat accomplished on 20 July 1969.

With the end of the Cold War following the fall of the Berlin Wall on 9 November 1989, former foes often joined forces as business partners in an ever-increasing

effort to exploit space for commercial purposes on Earth, particularly as regards satellite telephone communications, television and Earth observation for weather forecasting, regional planning and global navigation. Architects have participated in all these expanded opportunities for commercial space, from the 1990s remodelling of launch pads at Cape Canaveral by BRPH, and the redesign of Vandenburg Air Force Base by Bechtel for the accommodation of commercial satellite launches of Boeing's Delta II launchers, to the Austin Company's design of a new factory in Decatur, Alabama, for Boeing's next generation of Delta launchers.

Architects have also designed museums directly related to the Cold War, such as Leo Daly's striking new Strategic Air Command (SAC) Museum of 1998 in Ashland, Nebraska. The National Aeronautics and Space Administration (NASA) has had a team of

trained architects and specialists in human factors working on the design of the current international space station (ISS), scheduled for completion in 2004–05, and its predecessors since the mid-1980s. In addition, it has hired outside consultants to work on the space-station design. These include industrial designer John Frassanito, who worked with Raymond Loewy on the interiors of NASA's Skylab space station of 1967–73; architect Chas Willitts, now with NASA's aeronautics division; industrial designers Teague Associates, design consultants for Boeing commercial airliners from 1945; and, most recently, Houston architect Constance Adams. Since 1999, she has been developing ideas for Transhab, an inflatable structure to be used as a module of the ISS and, perhaps, for other buildings on future planetary missions. For the latter, Frassanito has developed, with NASA mission planners, scenarios for inflating a Transhab as part of the proposed human exploration of Mars.

Space tourism has become a buzz phrase for the new millennium, with various companies, small and large, proposing new vehicles to deliver satellites into orbit as well as to take visitors beyond Earth's gravitational pull. Architects from the Japanese construction company Shimizu and the Hawaii firm of Wimberly Allison Tong & Goo are proposing orbiting hotels as tourist destinations for these planned flights, which many believe will take place within the next decade or two. These have been well publicised in the media, interest fueled by the many who have already reserved places for these trips (recalling the thousands of similar reservations received by Pan Am after people saw their spaceliner in Stanley Kubrick's 1968 film *2001: A Space Odyssey*). But architects have not fully revealed how these massive structures would be built, nor how visitors and staff would react to a variety of potentially distressing situations in microgravity that would affect their bodily functions.

For now, however, theme parks such as the Star Trek Experience of 1998 at the Las Vegas Hilton by the Landmark Entertainment Group, or their planned Spacepark Bremen and similar structures such as the Starship Orion Casino designed by Hellmuth Obata and Kassabaum, will have to be our earthly substitutes for space architecture, just as they have in the past – Disney's rocket to the Moon in Tomorrowland of 1955 being among the most familiar. In any event, architects have always had an interest in shaping environments on Earth, whether or not they have worked on projects directly related to military, political or commercial uses of space. And it is certain that one day, when tourists travel into space, there will be architect-designed environments for them to inhabit, whether or not those spaces will be made in the same way as they are on Earth. ⌂

Above left
Frassanito & Associates, Designers. Still from an animation prepared for NASA, showing proposed inflatable Transhab as part of a Mars mission, c 1997–98.

Above right
The Landmark Entertainment Group, Architects. Entrance to the Star Trek Experience within the Hilton Hotel, Las Vegas, 1998.

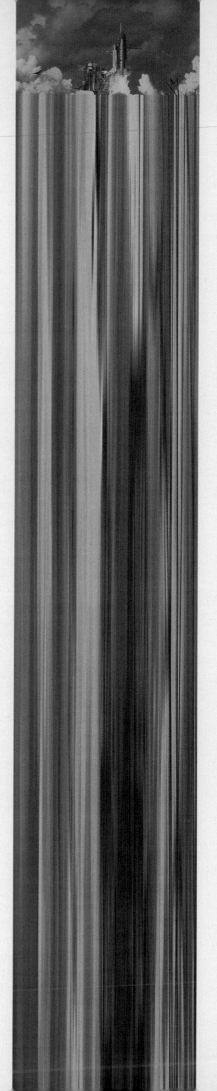

How Soon Will Space Tourism Start?

If at the beginning of the 20th century the question was whether man would ever be able to go into space, at the turn of the 21st century it is, when will people habitually be able to travel into space? David Ashford, Director of Bristol Spaceplanes Limited, shows how soon an infrastructure can be developed that will give the public access to orbit.

How soon is space tourism likely to start? Published estimates range from two years from now to 30 or more. Original analysis by Bristol Spaceplanes Limited indicates that suborbital tourism (brief flights that achieve just space height) will probably start in six or seven years.[1] Orbital tourism (flights that remain in space like a satellite) will start in about 10 years at a cost affordable only by the wealthy. In about 15 years, the cost will be reduced to a level affordable by middle-income people prepared to save. To explain this forecast, I will start by reviewing the engineering fundamentals and the business case, and then go on to consider possible time scales.

ENGINEERING FUNDAMENTALS
Design Requirements
From the reports of some 400 astronauts to date, we know that a trip to space is a fascinating experience. The main attractions are the views of the Earth, seeing the various heavenly bodies and playing around in microgravity. Thus, it seems likely that large numbers of people will want to go as soon as it is sufficiently safe and economical. At present, it costs more than $10 million to send someone into orbit, and that person's chance of a fatal accident during the trip is about one in 100. This compares with about one in a million for a flight in an airliner and one in 100,000 for a sporting parachute jump. Clearly, the main requirements for space tourism are vast improvements in the cost and safety of space transport.

Aeroplanes vs Ballistic Missiles
Why is current space travel so expensive and risky? Fig 1 summarises the development of US launch vehicles, from captured V-2 ballistic missiles up to the space shuttle. They are all based on ballistic missile technology, with large components that can fly only once. This is the basic cause of the high cost and risk of space flight to date. Even a mass-produced expendable launcher would cost too much for large-scale commercial use. Communication satellites are the only spacecraft to date that have been funded largely by the private sector. The resulting low launch rate of around 100 per year has prevented space transport from coming even close to the mature operations of an airline. Months or even years of preparation are required for each flight, involving armies of staff and mountains of paperwork. The shuttle has made fewer than 100 flights in 18 years.

Passenger aeroplanes, on the other hand, make more than 10 million flights per year worldwide. A new airliner design typically requires 1,000 test flights to just gain its type certificate for carrying passengers.

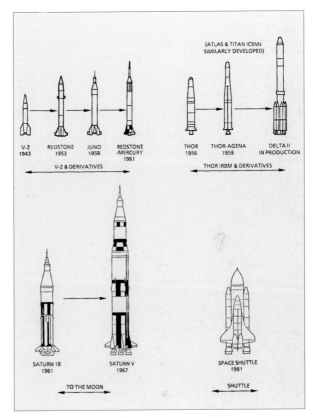

Figure 1
The basic cause of the high cost and high risk of space to date is the evolution of launch vehicles from missile technology. As a consequence, launch vehicles are still sent into orbit with large components that can be used for only a single flight.

To take the comparison with airline operations further, Fig 2 contrasts some fundamental aspects of the space shuttle with those of a large airliner. The shuttle is about 10,000 times more expensive per flight, and 10,000 times more risky.

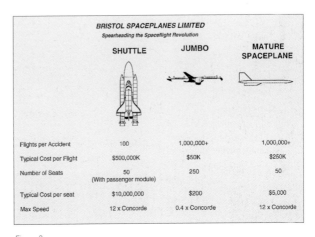

Figure 2
To make space tourism viable, a mature spaceplane needs to be developed that can carry passengers as regularly as an airliner.

In order to meet the requirements of space tourism, we will need to develop an airliner that can fly into orbit, that is, a mature spaceplane or spaceliner.

Space-tourism Infrastructure

In addition to spaceliners, we will need space hotels and heavy lift vehicles to launch them, fig 3. The idea of such a complete orbital infrastructure is by no means a new one. Wernher Von Braun and others were carrying out realistic studies in this area as early as the beginning of the 1950s.[2] NASA came close to achieving it 27 years ago with the Skylab space station, Saturn heavy lift vehicle and the X-15 suborbital spaceplane. However, they did not close the gap by developing an orbital successor to the X-15.

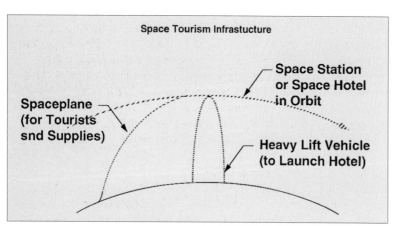

Space Tourism Infrastucture

Spaceplane (for Tourists snd Supplies)

Space Station or Space Hotel in Orbit

Heavy Lift Vehicle (to Launch Hotel)

Figure 3
To support hotels in orbit, an entire spacetourism infrastructure needs to be created. As well as requiring spaceliners to ferry passengers to the leisure complexes, heavy lift vehicles will be necessary to launch the hotels.

Mature vs Experimental

Experimental aeroplanes may be built if it is necessary to test or demonstrate new aerospace technologies. They may require much servicing between flights, may have a short life and will not be certified for carrying passengers or for operational military use. If successful, they should lead to a mature design that requires little servicing, has a long life and a type certificate for carrying passengers (or the military equivalent).

Typically, the cost of developing an experimental aeroplane is 10 per cent of the follow-on operational aeroplane. It can be virtually hand-built without full production drawings and tooling, and does not need test flights for certification.

For a spaceplane to achieve mature operations like those of airliners, with long life,

quick turnaround and low maintenance costs, the key engineering developments are durable and cheap to maintain rocket motors, thermal protection, and transparencies. The development of these long-life systems would take around 10 years of in-service experience and incremental, detailed improvement, assuming a major development effort. The other systems in the spaceplane can be based on existing aeroplane technology.

Suborbital vs Orbital

Fig 4 compares suborbital with orbital flights. Suborbital flights are easier to achieve because the maximum speed required is far lower (around Mach 4 compared with Mach 25). The required fuel weight is thereby much less (about 50 per cent of take-off weight compared with around 87 per cent for a single-stage-to-orbit vehicle with the most efficient rocket motors available). Thus, the least expensive way to demonstrate the potential for aeroplane-like space operations is to build a small suborbital spaceplane. And the easiest way to build a fully orbital spaceplane is to use two stages. The lower stage, or carrier aeroplane, takes the upper stage, or orbiter, to high speed and height and releases it to carry on to satellite speed. With careful design, the technology required for each stage need not be much more advanced than that of a suborbital spaceplane.

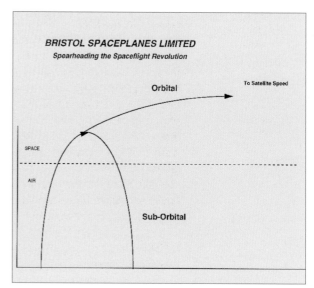

BRISTOL SPACEPLANES LIMITED
Spearheading the Spaceflight Revolution

To Satellite Speed

Orbital

SPACE

AIR

Sub-Orbital

Figure 4
Sub-orbital spaceplanes can be far smaller than orbital ones, and are the least expensive way of showing the business potential of space tourism.

Space Hotels

The technology for space hotels already exists, as demonstrated by several successful space stations. However, four factors make present space stations extremely expensive: novelty, high political profile, low production rate and the fact that the call-out charge for a plumber or electrician to fix a failure is some $500 million, the approximate cost of a space shuttle launch. These factors lead to vehicles designed on a one-off basis to standards far more demanding than those of aeroplanes.

Given low-cost access on demand by mature spaceplanes, none of these factors need apply and space stations could soon reach the maturity required to serve as hotels. They would then cost roughly the same as airliners of comparable size. A space station with the internal volume of a Boeing 747, for example, would cost around $200 million. The international space station, at present under development, will cost some $50 billion, which is 250 times more expensive. This is a measure of the cost-penalty of building large space stations before assuring low-cost access to orbit. The development of low-cost space hotels therefore depends on low-cost access on demand, which in turn depends on the development of mature spaceplanes.

Heavy Lift Vehicles

Large space hotels will be launched as modules to be assembled in orbit. Each module is launched once only and will have a life of more than 20 years. Thus, the cost per flight of the heavy lift vehicle is far less significant than that of the spaceplane, which has to fly something like 1,000 times more frequently if we assume a supply flight every few days. Existing large launchers, such as the space shuttle or Ariane, could be used if necessary, although their cost could be greatly reduced by applying technology from the mature spaceplane.

Safety

It should be possible to develop spaceplanes to the same safety level as airliners. There are, however, four new or increased hazards: radiation, space debris, re-entry heating, and the far worse effects of cabin depressurisation. These risks should be manageable in the same way that other transport risks are managed, that is, by sound engineering practice, minimising exposure, shielding, system redundancy, highly trained staff, adequate regulation, statistical analysis and painstaking, detailed development.

Adequate safety cannot be achieved with expendable launchers. They can fly only once, and therefore cannot be tested in flight before delivery. Very few development flights can be afforded, compared with the 1,000 or so test flights needed before a new airliner design gains its type certificate for carrying passengers.

Potential Cost

The cost per seat to orbit in a mature spaceliner would be around $5,000.[3] This is considerably higher than that for a long-distance flight in an airliner, due to the fact that the spaceliner needs a far higher fuel load. This is both expensive in its own right and reduces the number of people it can carry. Moreover, a spaceliner designed for early maturity would be more complicated than present airliners because of the two stages outlined above. Simpler, single-stage spaceliners could follow a few years later, but will need advanced engines and structures.

A preliminary estimate of the total cost of a space holiday suggests that the spaceplane cost will be some 70 per cent of the total.[4] Thus, including the cost of the hotel, profits and overheads, it seems probable that the fare for a few days in space will be around $10,000, affordable by middle-income people prepared to save. It is 1,000 times less than the present cost of sending people to space, and requires just a combination of reusability and airliner maturity.

BUSINESS CASE
Market

Market research carried out in Japan suggests that around one million people per year from that country alone would pay $10,000 for a few days in a space hotel.[5] Subsequent surveys in Canada and the US indicate a comparable fraction of the population prepared to pay that amount.[6] Assuming that this is true worldwide, the total annual demand for space tourism at a cost of $10,000 could be as high as 15 million people – the Japanese gross domestic product is about 1/15th of the world total. However, given the limitations of market surveys for a product that requires much imagination to appreciate, it would be prudent for business planning to assume an initial annual demand of just one million space tourists. Even this would require a fleet of around 50 spaceplanes of 50-seat capacity, each making one flight per day. The total market would be about $10 billion, which is more than in any present use of space.

One million people per year is equivalent to 7.5 per cent of the industrialised population (assumed here to be one billion) making one flight per lifetime (assumed to be 75 years). This seems a conservative estimate of the demand for a unique and transforming experience at a cost of a few months' income, particularly since most people anticipate that they would wish to go more than once.[7]

Finance

The achievement of a mature orbital infrastructure will require a large and expensive development effort not justified at present by the satellite-launch market. Since the most credible large-scale new space business is tourism, the funding of a mature orbital infrastructure depends on the business case. An economic analysis of the build-up of a space-tourism industry, based on realistic estimates of the market, costs and revenues, shows a good return on investment.[8] The market for space tourism is substantial enough to provide both the operating experience and the commercial incentive to achieve maturity within a reasonable time scale.

First, however, a catch-22 must be overcome. Low-cost space transportation depends on maturity, whose development depends in turn on a commercial incentive, which depends on high traffic levels, which depends in turn on space tourism! It is therefore not practicable to gain the required development funding in one go: an incremental approach is necessary.

HOW SOON COULD SPACE TOURISM START?
Development Strategy

In order to break into this circular situation, Bristol Spaceplanes Limited has worked up a development strategy based on a logic that links up the basic engineering and market factors described above.

The goal is to develop a mature spaceplane at minimum cost and risk. Mature spaceplanes will slash the cost of ferrying people to and from space, and will enable the development of low-cost space stations and heavy lift vehicles. They will transform the whole culture of space transport into that of an airline business. To reach maturity as soon as practicable, the design should use more-or-less existing technology and therefore requires two stages. The spaceplane also needs to be piloted, in order to meet the safety standards for carrying passengers.

Spacebus is a 50-seater that could achieve the $10,000 cost target. A prototype could be built in five years with existing technology. It would be suitable for launching satellites and supplying space stations, but would have a short life and high maintenance cost. Even so, it would be far less expensive to fly than expendable launchers. To achieve airliner-like maturity would take about 10 years of incremental development. Thus, space tourism could become big business in about 15 years.

Although it would be possible to develop Spacebus in one go, a step-by-step approach is needed, for the reasons mentioned earlier. As the next step, we have selected the least expensive project that will demonstrate the business potential of space tourism and thereby enable the remaining funding to be obtained: a prototype of a small, piloted, suborbital spaceplane.

Ascender (fig. 6) takes off and climbs to about 30,000 feet using jet engines. Its rocket then takes over and pulls it up into a near vertical accelerating climb, from which it can coast to 60 miles high.

BRISTOL SPACEPLANES LIMITED
Spearheading the Spaceflight Revolution

Spaceplane Development Strategy

Ascender	Spacecab	Spacebus
4 Seat Sub-orbital Spaceplane (Re-Invented X-15)	6 Seat or One Tonne Orbital Spaceplane Piloted, Two Stage, HTOHL	50 Seat or Five Tonne Orbital Spaceplane Piloted, Two Stage, HTOHL
£50 million D&D	£600 million D&D	
Research Applications, then Sub-Orbital Tourism	Small Satellites Space Station Supply Orbital Tourism	Mature Tourism £6,000 per trip
First Flight in 3 Years	First Flight in 5 Years	Airliner Maturity in 15 Years

Figure 5
The potential market for space tourism is large enough – approximately one million people in Japan alone – to provide the commercial incentive for investment. The most practical way of making a mature spaceplane a reality is through an incremental approach.

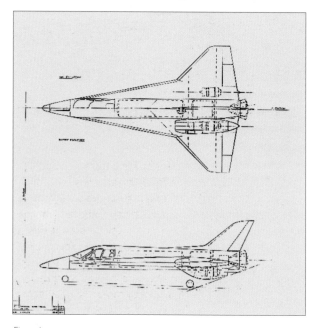

Figure 6
Ascender is a small, piloted, suborbital spaceplane designed by British Spaceplanes Limited – the first step towards space tourism. Within 6 to 7 years, the spaceplane could be certified to carry a pair of passengers with a crew of two.

Ascender would be used initially as a reusable sounding rocket for space research and as a spaceplane technology test-bed. After a few years in service, it would be certificated for carrying a pair of passengers with a crew of two. Passengers would experience a couple of minutes of microgravity, could view an area the size of England at one time and would see the sky turn black with bright stars even in daytime. Designed for fast turnaround at low maintenance cost, Ascender is conceived as a method of initiating an embryonic space-tourism business. The aeroplane closest to Ascender in terms of basic engineering is the Saunders-Roe SR53 jet plus rocket fighter, which first flew in 1957 (fig. 7). The two are of broadly comparable size and weight, and both have a jet engine and a rocket motor. Only two prototypes of the SR53 were built, and it did not enter service. Had it done so, its cost per flight would probably not have been very different from that of modern jet fighters, which is typically around $10,000. This provides a preliminary target for the cost per flight of Ascender when mature.

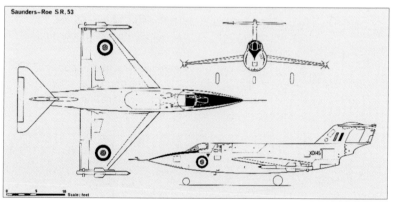

Figure 7
The aeroplane that provides the closest model for the Ascender is the Saunders-Roe SR53 jet plus rocket fighter, first flown in 1957.

A prototype of Ascender could be flying in three years time, and could be certificated for carrying passengers three or four years later, after a few hundred flights to demonstrate safety and reliability. Suborbital space tourism could therefore begin in six or seven years.

The next step, Spacecab, is shown in Fig 8. It is designed to be the smallest two-stage spaceplane that can carry a large enough payload to capture a good share of the existing launcher business. It can launch a one ton satellite, or carry six passengers or space-station crew. A feasibility study for the European Space Agency (ESA) showed that a Spacecab prototype could be built with existing engines

and proven materials.[9] Such a prototype could be completed in five years and would be used for launching small satellites and servicing space stations. Since it would need about five years of operational experience to demonstrate the safety needed for carrying passengers, orbital tourism could start 10 years from now. The fare level would be high, and these early trips would be affordable only by the wealthy.

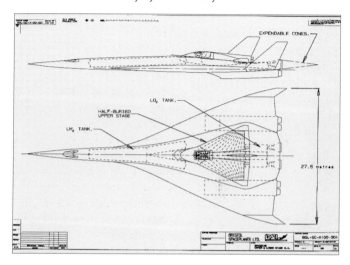

Figure 8
Spacecab is a small, two-stage spaceplane that could carry six passengers. Given backing, it could be built to launch small satellites and service small stations within 5 years.

The development cost of Spacecab to the point of early operational flights carrying non-passenger payloads is some $1 billion, which is about the cost of just two shuttle flights.[10] It would therefore pay for itself by replacing the shuttle for a very few missions. This would provide the basis for asking government space agencies to guarantee the purchase of enough launches, at a lower cost than they would otherwise have to pay using existing expendable launchers, so that the private sector could fund Spacecab's development. NASA and ESA would thereby save money and help slash the cost of access to space

Spaceplane History

The above analysis suggests that (in round, conservative figures) a fleet of 50 spaceplanes carrying one million people each year at a fare of $10,000 each is a realistic goal for space policy to aim at. The forecast that it could be achieved in 15 years may seem optimistic, but a look at aerospace history suggests that this milestone could actually have been achieved several years ago. We have seen that the first step in replacing expendable launchers with spaceplanes should be a suborbital spaceplane. Well, the first of these was tested 40 years ago. The X-15 (fig. 9) was an experimental suborbital spaceplane that first flew in 1959 and made 199 flights before the project was abandoned in 1968. It is generally thought to have been one of the most successful research aeroplanes yet built.

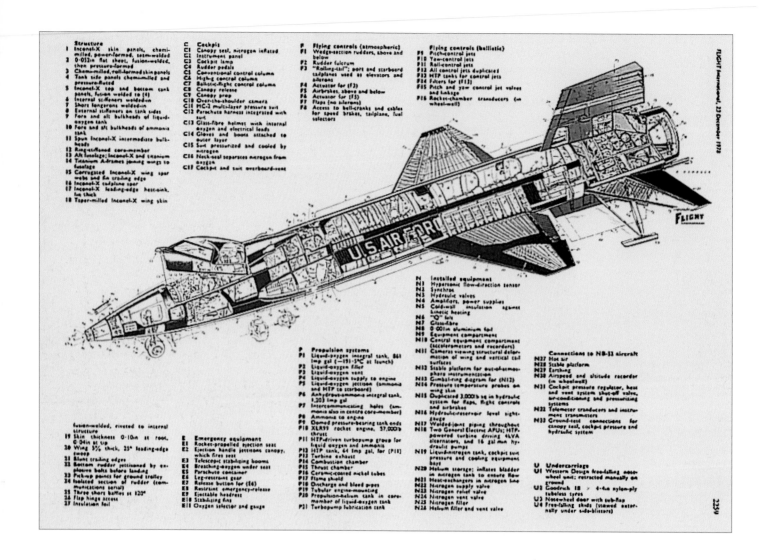

The cutaway drawing is labelled throughout with a detailed key describing the structure, cockpit, flying controls (atmospheric), flying controls (ballistic), propulsion systems, emergency equipment, installed equipment, connections to NB-52 aircraft, and undercarriage of the X-15 aircraft.

Figure 9
The first step towards space tourism, the development of the spaceplane, was taken over 40 years ago with the X-15, an experimental suborbital spaceplane that made 199 flights before it was abandoned in 1968.

Bristol Spaceplanes Limited was initiated by myself in 1991. I had started professional life working on spaceplanes with the Hawker Siddeley Aviation Advanced Projects Group in 1961. At the time, the X-15 was flying ever higher and faster, and was the inspiration for the spaceplane work of most of the large aerospace companies in Europe and the US. We were sure that spaceplanes were the logical next step in space transport and that they were feasible. A two-stage orbital successor to the X-15 could have entered service launching small satellites and supplying space stations by the mid-1970s because, as mentioned earlier, the technology for each stage need not be much more advanced than that required for a suborbital spaceplane. Allowing 20 years for the technology to mature, space tourism would probably by now have become a large-scale business. This is not just hindsight. Several spaceplane proponents in the 1960s envisaged their eventual use for carrying passengers, although at that time the favoured

application was long-range, high-speed transport rather than space tourism.

So why have orbital spaceplanes never been developed? The Cold War is largely responsible. Due to the resulting pressures, the first men in space got there on top of converted ballistic missiles, starting in 1960. Before then, it had been widely expected that high-speed rocket spaceplanes would be used, developed from the sequence of research aeroplanes starting with the winged V-2 of 1945 and leading to the X-15 via the X-1, Skyrocket and X-2. These pioneering manned space flights were followed by the race to the Moon, which the USA won in 1969 using large expendable launchers. Reusability would not have greatly reduced cost because of the small number of flights involved, and would have delayed the programme. By then, the habit of sending people up using ballistic missile technology had stuck, and the next major project, the space shuttle, was not fully reusable. With its expendable large propellant tank and recyclable solid rocket boosters, it is as expensive and as risky as the expendable vehicles that preceded it. The compelling

Notes

1 D M Ashford, 'Space Tourism – How Soon Will It Happen?', paper presented at IEEE Aerospace Conference, Snowmass, Colorado, 1–8 Feb 1997. (Downloadable from www.bristolspaceplanes.com.)
2 Wernher von Braun, 'Prelude to Space Travel', in Cornelius Ryan (ed), *Across the Space Frontier*, Sidgwick and Jackson, (London), 1952.
3 The analysis behind this estimate is given in the text referred to in note 1, which covers much the same ground as this article but in greater technical detail.
4 Ashford, 'A Development Strategy for Space Tourism', JBIS, February 1997, first presented at 46th International Astronautical Congress, Oslo, October 1995.
5 Patrick Collins, Yoichi Iwasaki, Hideki Hanayama and Misuzu Ohnuki, 'Commercial Implications of Market Research on Space Tourism', *Journal of Space Technology and Science*, vol 10, no 2, pp 3–11.
6 P Collins, R Stockmans and M Maita, 'Demand for Space Tourism in America and Japan, and its Implications for Future Space Activities', presented at Sixth International Space Conference of Pacific-Basin Societies, Marina del Rey, California, December 1995.
7 Collins, Iwasaki, Hanayama and Ohnuki, 'Commercial Implications', op cit.
8 Ashford, 'A Development Strategy', op cit.
9 'A Preliminary Feasibility Study of the Spacecab Low-Cost Spaceplane and of the Spacecab Demonstrator', Bristol Spaceplanes Limited Report TR 6, February 1994. Carried out under European Space Agency contract no 10411/93/F/TB. Vol 1 reproduced as 'The Potential of Spaceplanes' in *Journal of Practical Applications in Space*, Spring 1995.
10 Ashford, 'Space Tourism – How Sonn Will it Happen?', op cit.
11 'General Public Space Travel and Tourism', NASA/STA joint study, NP-1998-03-11-MSFC, March 1998. (Downloadable from www.spacefuture.com.).

Websites
Bristol Spaceplanes Limited: www.bristolspaceplanes.com
Space Tourism: www.spacefuture.com

arguments in favour of a small but fully reusable launcher were swamped by the politics of a new mega project.

This brief consideration of spaceplane history shows that the feasibility of an aeroplane like Ascender is not in doubt. It is a sort of reinvented X-15, taking advantage of the subsequent 40 years of technology to provide everyday aeroplane-like operations. The X-15 flew as high and as fast. By using the higher performance engines now available, however, Ascender avoids the need for air-launch and is smaller. Employing external thermal protection updated and simplified from that developed for the shuttle, Ascender can use a conventional aluminium alloy airframe. Systems for life support, reaction controls, communication and navigation are all well within the state of the art.

In aerospace history, the time scale from a record-breaking experimental aeroplane to operational deployment of the new capability has usually been less than 10 years. Suborbital spaceplanes were abandoned with the last flight of the X-15 in 1968. A rapid catching up is possible.

US Developments

In the US, several spaceplanes are at last under development. NASA are part-funding the X-33 and X-34 experimental vehicles, which are due to fly this year. Several private US start-up companies, notably Kelly Aerospace, Kistler Aerospace, Pioneer Rocketplane and Rotary Rocket, have gained significant funding to initiate the development of reusable launchers. It is highly probable that at least one of these US developments will lead to an operational reusable launch vehicle within five years. Adding the 10 years required to achieve maturity, space tourism could be a large-scale business within 15 years. This time scale is consistent with that of the Bristol Seaplanes Limited strategy outlined above, and the result would be similar. However, if the logic behind the strategy is correct, the US projects all have higher cost and risk. May the market choose.

Probable Time Scale

The challenge is essentially that of overcoming the credibility barrier to obtaining the required investment. A strong rational case can be made for investing in space tourism, but the proposed developments are so out of line with present official policy that it is difficult to persuade venture capitalists to take the idea seriously. My personal view, based on the experience of several years of

trying to gain backing, is that it will take an aeroplane flying regularly to space to change the mindset.

This is the motivation behind the X-Prize (see p 34), a $10 million award for the first team to build a suborbital spaceplane capable of carrying three people. (I hope that the winner will be Ascender, but wish the competition the best of luck.) The first spaceplane to achieve routine space flights could either be Ascender, or one of the US reusable launchers, or one of the X-Prize contenders. The winner will probably be the first to succeed in raising the funds, which is the main preoccupation at present of spaceplane purveyors.

Whichever wins, it will look and fly like an aeroplane. The idea that with further development it could also carry passengers as an aeroplane does will then seem entirely reasonable. Marketeers will no doubt point out that all that is needed to achieve a thousandfold reduction in the cost of sending people into orbit is maturity, and private-sector funding sources would then start to take seriously the business case for space tourism. NASA and ESA will then have a choice between supporting space tourism and being sidelined. NASA have carried out a joint feasibility study of space tourism with the Space Transportation Association (STA), which has positive conclusions, and may be starting to follow up the policy implications.[11]

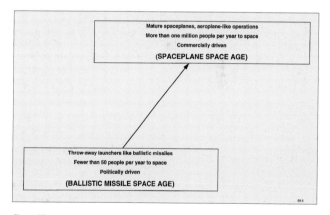

Figure 10
With two experimental spaceplanes part-funded by NASA due to fly this year, the efforts of several start-up companies, and the incentive of the $10 million X-prize, the early 21st century promises to be the Spaceplane Space Age.

Thus it seems likely that space tourism will start soon after the earliest practicable date, which is the basis for the forecast in the opening paragraph. Sub-orbital tourism will therefore probably start in six or seven years, leading to a paradigm shift in astronautics, with launchers based on aeroplane technology replacing those based on ballistic missiles. This revolution is comparable to that in aeronautics 100 years ago, when the invention of the aeroplane led to the rapid replacement of balloons for most purposes, and to an explosive growth in demand. Balloons cannot fly into wind. Ballistic missiles cannot fly more than once. In each case, aeroplanes provide the solution. ⌀

Space Tourism – the Key to the Coming Economic Boom

In the post-Cold War world, government agencies have lost the competitive incentive of the East–West space race, and the future of space travel is shifting towards the free market. Patrick Collins, Vice President of Spacetopia and guest researcher at NASDA (the Japanese space agency), considers the increasing economic feasibility of a space-tourism industry.

Most people dismiss the possibility of space tourism. This is, however, to overlook today's greatest business opportunity. Tourism in space, travelling at first to just a few hundred kilometres above the Earth, and then on to the Moon, is going to start within just a few years and looks set to grow explosively to more than $100 billion a year over the next three decades. To dispel popular prejudices, this article contests five of the most commonly held preconceptions holding back space tourism, before considering the economic imperatives propelling it forwards.

'If it were possible, NASA would be doing it.'
This common response to the idea of ordinary people going into space completely misunderstands the historical preoccupations of NASA. NASA was set up during the Cold War to compete with the Soviet Union's government space agency in 'space development and exploration'; other countries set up space agencies, notably the European Space Agency ESA and the Japanese NASDA, to follow suit. With the end of the Cold War, the agencies have interpreted their roles to mean scientific and engineering research in space, excluding commercial development.

The government space agencies of the world currently spend $25 billion of taxpayers' money every year - but almost none of their activities is of any value in achieving the objective of enabling 'ordinary people' – that is, you and me, who pay for all these activities – to go into space ourselves. For example, less than 2 per cent of NASA's budget is devoted to work on reusable launch vehicles, and the figure is less than 0.2 per cent in the case of ESA or NASDA.

What has changed recently is that, having loftily dismissed the idea of 'non-astronautic space travel' for decades, nasa has now admitted, in print, that space tourism is feasible – it could start within just a few years, and it is likely to become the major commercial activity in space.

The report that blew the gaff, entitled 'General Public Space Travel and Tourism', was published by NASA and the Washington-based Space Transportation Association (STA), which has been concerned for years about the lack of growth in the launch business. Tourism is the only really promising new market - just as promising as tourism on Earth, which is the largest, fastest growing industry in the world economy, turning over several trillion dollars per year, and employing approximately 10 per cent of the world's working population.

The NASA administrator Daniel Goldin has started to refer to space tourism occasionally in his speeches, but most NASA staff still see their future as government-funded. Tellingly, the report mentioned above is not available through NASA's website.

What is most frustrating is that there is actually no need for government space agencies to operate space-tourism services themselves. Indeed, private companies should certainly be the ones to do it. In addition, in view of the 'wall of money' available in global capital markets, there should be no problem financing rapid growth in the industry. For example, once Japanese companies came to see the promise of mobile telephones they quickly invested $30 billion, creating a boom in which 40 million people bought mobile phones within just three years, and generating $40 billion a year turnover in a single country. Therefore, from the financial point of view, the development of space tourism worldwide over 15 years is easy. However, as with all new ideas, the essential step is to persuade investors that they are credible. And guess what space entrepreneurs hear when they go to talk to investors? 'This sounds very interesting – we'll just ask NASA what they think.' Asking NASA's opinion about space tourism is, however, like asking the air force about the cost of holiday flights. This means that nasa staff-members' opinions on space tourism can be less than useful, but unfortunately they still tend to be treated as gospel. As a result, companies that are trying to raise money, like Rotary Rocket Inc and Bristol Spaceplanes Limited, are currently constrained to minute budgets when compared to that of space agencies.

From market research, it is known that space-tourism services will be immensely popular, but most people, including investors, still have no idea how feasible they are. Additional publicity is therefore needed to put pressure on governments to be more constructive towards the founding of this promising new industry.

'Even if it were possible, it could only ever be for the rich.'

If you asked your grandparents whether they thought as children that they would ever fly in an aeroplane, they'd probably say something like, 'Oh no, I never dreamed of it. Flying was just for Hollywood stars and politicians!' The phrase 'the jet set' is an indication of how unobtainable international travel was even till quite recently.

The truth is that space travel should not be fundamentally less accessible than air travel to the general public. With a focused plan to produce a passenger space vehicle, suborbital passenger flights like that made by the first American in space, Alan Shepard, could start within just a few years. In addition, once they

begin, you can rely on business to do what it does best of all - drive prices down, grow the market and develop new services. Studies have shown that in that case, within a couple of decades, turnover could reach around one million passengers per year, and prices could be around $25,000 for a short orbital trip. At that price, bearing in mind that average incomes will nearly double over the next 20 years, essentially all the middle classes will be able to take a trip. For example, anyone who saves the equivalent of $100 a month should be able to take a trip within 20 years from now.

If some readers are sceptical as to whether such a 'low' price is obtainable, it may be worth noting that the physical energy needed to carry a person into orbit (that is, to accelerate them to a speed of 8 kilometres per second) costs just several tens of dollars. Space travel only remains, in part, expensive today because a rocket has to carry not only passengers but also all its fuel (or 'propellants' as rocket engineers say), which has roughly 100 times the mass of the passengers. In addition, currently all rockets, except for part of the us space shuttle, are 'expendable' – used only once. By contrast, a Boeing 747 is used about 50,000 times before it is scrapped, which significantly reduces the cost per flight.

'Only superfit people can go to space.'

The first astronauts and cosmonauts were military pilots, because no one knew for sure what risks they might face. However, it quickly became clear that the only risk they faced was the failure of the vehicles in which they were travelling. Everything else was fine and predictable – even the radiation in space.

The lengthy selection and training process of NASA staff has preserved the idea that ordinary people cannot tolerate the 'rigours' of space flight. But this is a myth - there are no rigours. The only reason for the elaborate selection and training is that space-shuttle flights are extremely expensive – several hundred millions of dollars each. Consequently, if one of the crew were to fall ill or to work inefficiently, this would waste a huge amount of money.

The truth is that space flight is extremely relaxing; many people in orbit find they need to sleep only a few hours a night. And so long as you're lying on your back, the 3 g acceleration that you feel for about five minutes when going into orbit and coming back is nothing - it feels like having a small baby on your chest. It is far less stressful than riding a modern roller coaster, for example.

Therefore, although the earliest passenger rides to space may still require customers to do some training in case of emergencies, within a decade or so there will scarcely be more restrictions on who can go into orbit than there are on who can fly on an aeroplane. There will, however, be a need for some guidelines for spaceline passengers because a number of issues are different from those involved in air travel. One is that the amount of radiation in low Earth orbit is more than that within the atmosphere, and so a passenger spending a few days in orbit will receive as much radiation as most people receive in a year on the ground (from X-rays, etc). This is still a tiny amount, and of no significant danger. Another issue is that people with heart disease may be at greater risk, since the body's fluids are redistributed in zero gravity. A third problem is that some medicines have less effect in zero gravity than they do on Earth, and therefore some passengers will need to take precautionary advice. The Federal Aviation Administration (FAA) in the usa is already preparing a draft version of such guidelines for space-travel companies to issue to customers.

For those who want to stay longer in space – perhaps working for a month or two as hotel staff in orbit – a two-month tour of duty in low orbit will bring their dose up to the level of 'radiation workers' on Earth.

'Everyone who goes to space throws up – who'd pay to do that?'

Approximately half the people who have travelled on the space shuttle are said to have vomited within the first few hours of their trip. The equivalent of seasickness, it is effectively treated by anti-motion-sickness medication.

'Maybe it will be possible in a hundred years.'

If the development of space tourism is made an immediate priority, within as few as 30 years it could evolve into a large-scale international industry, generating employent for as many as 10 million people worldwide. The presence of visitors and through traffic would create a demand in orbit for a wide range of goods and services (including water from the Moon), providing further commercial opportunities for a range of aerospace and other companies; through the establishment of low-cost transport further business opportunities would be opened up in space – notably supplying solar energy to Earth using microwave power beams.

Yet the investment needed to create such a cornucopia of new economic opportunities is far less than the $750 billion that government space agencies will spend over the next 30 years if they continue their current activities – and all but the first billion dollars or so could come from private industry, not from taxpayers.

Space agencies dispose of large amounts of money operating throwaway rockets that cost hundreds of millions per flight because they do not have any need of the huge capacity that a fully reusable launch system offers (and indeed, needs, in order to be economical). Tourism offers an almost unlimited potential market, and can easily pay for the development of the necessary reusable systems – just as it has paid for the Boeing 747, big jet engines, and airlines' global computer networks. However, in the face of resistance from space agencies, it cannot get started.

It is worth noting that even at the rate of five million passengers per year (less than half a per cent of airline traffic, even today), still only a fraction of the middle classes of 2030 will have made a trip. This would indicate that the business could obviously grow significantly faster than already indicated. Looking at the longer term, with economic growth of 2.5 per cent a year – salaries double on average in 30 years and grow by a factor of 10 times over a century – by 2100, average incomes in the developed countries will be about $250,000 a year. This is sufficient for trips to and from space to be as commonplace as international air travel today (more than 1 billion passengers annually) and for a potential 100 million families to take trips to the Moon each year.

The big picture is that humans are out-growing Earth. As the world population doubles again over the coming decades, accessing the unlimited room to expand beyond Earth will become increasingly attractive.

Economic Imperative

It is unquestionable that the development of a space-tourism industry as described above will be extremely beneficial for world economic growth, which is currently experiencing 20-30 per cent over-capacity in a range of global industries – automobiles, steel, petro-chemicals, memory-chips and others. At the present, the development of the Internet is minimising its full impact. This is only in the short term, though, as Internet businesses are making existing work such as retailing more efficient, and will therefore in time destroy more jobs than they create. Tourism is already one of the largest industries in the world, employing 10 per cent of the working population. The only factor preventing tourism from expanding out into space and generating millions of new jobs in every sector of the economy is – specifically – the will to shift some small part of the $25 billion that taxpayers pay every year for non-profit-making space activities towards creating a new industry in space tourism.

The phrase 'post-Cold War era' is beginning to date. The truth is that we are on the brink of the real Space Age: that is, when we all get a chance to take a first step out into space, and the vast arena of our future. ◊

Website
www.spacefuture.com/archive/
space_activities_space_tourism
_and_economic_growth.shtml

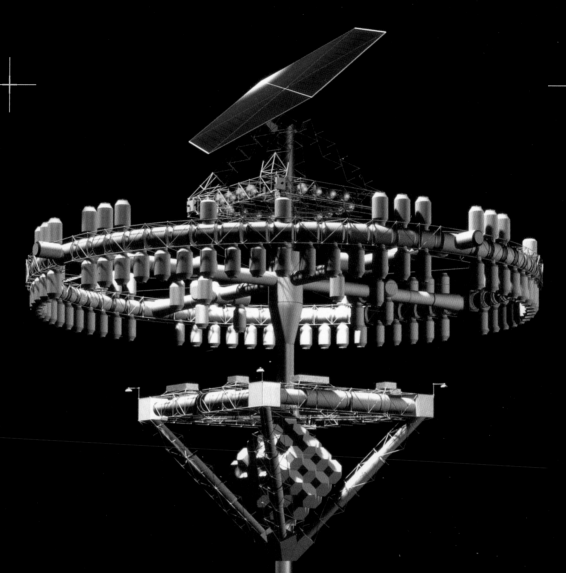

A new Era of Space Medicine for

Space Tourism

Architects designing for space have to ensure that they are fully able to anticipate the different physical demands that space travel puts on people's bodies. Here Kazuyoshi Yajima of the University of Nihon, the founder of the only space-medicine course in the world, gives a brief history of the special requirements for health care in orbit.

Almost 40 years have passed since the first human ventured into space. Looking back over this period, one could characterise the first decade of space flight by the race between the Soviet Union and the United States to dominate manned space flight. At that time, the challenge was in launching bigger manned satellites on the one hand, and in planting the first footprint on the surface of the Moon on the other. The second decade, the age of Skylab, Apollo–Soyuz and successive activities, witnessed a compromise between the two superpowers, due to the heavy economic weight their national budgets placed on space development. The third decade is defined by the space shuttle missions initiated by Columbia, heralding the age of reusable spacecraft. Sadly, the progressive development of these missions in the US was interrupted by the tragedy of Challenger. However, the Soviet Union, unaffected by this disaster, launched Mir, aiming at establishing a permanent space station in orbit.

1999. Meanwhile, in Japan, J-1, M-5, H-1 and H-2 rockets were developed. The next decade will be celebrated with the launch of the ISS, which is almost entirely funded by NASA, with other countries playing only a small part in its development; the US will therefore adopt the role of rich landlord to poor tenants.

It is likely that in future decades we will witness the establishment of space tourism. The spaceship Kankoh-Maru, designed by the Japanese Rocket Society and built by Kawasaki Heavy Industry, is just one example of an orbital craft that will be ready to meet the first wave of tourist excursions. It will hold 50 passengers at an altitude of 100 to 150 kilometres for at least four hours – time for almost two orbits around the Earth. Current estimates suggest that this excursion will cost $25,000 per person. Shimizu Corporation is also planning a space hotel to accommodate tourists for several days, at a rate of about $180,000 per person. These unique adventures are still prohibitively expensive for the average passenger: experts estimate that there are currently only about 50,000 people who could afford the hotel experience.

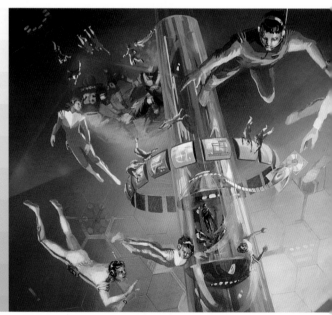

The last decade of space history began with worldwide chaos: the unification of Germany, the Gulf War and the collapse of the Soviet Union. The Japanese market economy 'bubble' also collapsed, which had a huge impact both on the rest of Asia and world markets in general. Consequently, government funding to NASA was squeezed and labour on the space programme reduced. However, NASA continued to prepare for the launch of its trophy space project, the international space station (ISS), and despite the poor state of its national economy Russia succeeded in maintaining Mir until the end of

When such projects are realised, health care and medicine in space will require skills completely different from established practices on Earth. Cosmonauts and astronauts face a challenging selection process and subsequently undergo rigorous training. They are superfit and healthy, both physically and mentally. During missions, the action of these athletes in microgravity is examined. Many physiological changes to astronauts have been recorded in space and in ground-simulation training. These include motion sickness, changes in neurovestibular functions, alteration in the higher brain functions, oedema, fluid shift, modification of reflexes, regulation in the cardiovascular system, muscle atrophy, continuous loss of bone minerals and changes in circadian rhythm. Also to be taken into consideration are the effects of cosmic radiation on the organs, a long-term stay in a closed, isolated and narrow space and mental stress due to the multicultural diversity of crew members and the radically different life style, values and diet in orbit. Discussed in terms of adaptation and inadaptation to microgravity, these problems have been studied at length and the countermeasures necessary to prevent them have been implemented and evaluated during space missions. Today, the primary role of space medicine is to investigate the speed of adaptation in microgravity in order to increase the performance of the crew. Other areas of space medicine include preventing the spread of infections to exclude pathogens such as any viruses from the craft.

From experience, space physicians know that the results of physiological changes in astronauts are not fatal if sustained for a period of only three to six months. But as far as I am aware, no one has stayed longer than a year in space. NASA is now planning to send six astronauts to Mars in 2014. It will take Pathfinder six months to reach the planet for a 14-month stay on the Martian surface, and another six months to return. The question of providing fuel, food, air, water and medical care over this lengthy period has yet to be solved. Additionally, the information to which we have access in terms of medical care in space applies only to healthy astronauts, not to people who may have diseases. In the history of 40 years of manned space flight, no astronaut has been reported seriously sick in space – there are no reports of operations in orbit, no injections, blood or fluid transfusion administered, and probably no bone fractures sustained.

With the advent of space tourism, the random cross section of ordinary people on board a spaceship will not have been through a medical checkup and will have had no physical training, just as they would not have had on an airline either. They may have a variety of common medical complaints such as colds, flu, diarrhoea, infectious diseases, hypertension or diabetes. Others may wish to travel precisely because they are ill – patients in the terminal stages of cancer, for example, or elderly people wanting to see the Earth from space before incapacity, senescence or death. Spaceship doctors will be responsible for the safe return of these tourists. Although many flights will be launched without

incident, there is a significant probability that the need to treat a patient in space will occur. In the case of our established modes of transport such as planes or trains emergency landings and stops can be made, but on an expensive space tour this may be impossible. Even for a short period of four or five hours, there is a significant risk of a serious or difficult situation occurring. But the fact that the need to perform emergency medical procedures in space has never arisen creates a serious problem: we do not know how to stop bleeding or sew up injured skin in zero gravity, or what to do in space when tiny bubbles appear in a syringe.

What kinds of medicine can we offer to space tourists? A large number of airlines carry a defibrillator and basic medical emergency kit on board, but they do not provide a doctor. It is likely that at least one doctor will accompany each space tour, but what is the optimum number of medically trained people per flight? What sort of precautions should be taken to ensure safety in space for ordinary, sick or weak people, at least for the several hours they will spend in zero and hypergravity at launch and re-entry? What advice should be given to those who have chronic illnesses who wish to see Earth from space in their lifetime? What should be the procedure if the majority of passengers begin to vomit? Where can doctors receive training in skills such as performing operations and giving injections in changing gravitational fields? Although doctors are traditionally required to study as specialists, in space they will be expected to have diverse skills ranging from internal medicine to surgery, orthopaedics, psychiatry and dermatology. How can we educate such 'super doctors'?

By the time doctors are routine crew members on spaceships, it is also probable that telemedicine will be an established way of training and communication between doctors. This form of remote medical instruction will be based on communications technologies and, fortuitously, the most advanced computer-aided design (CAD) systems in existence are likely to be part of the technology already on board the spaceship. Telemedicine will provide a two-way channel for spaceship doctors to contact hospitals on Earth in an emergency. But even experts may be baffled by some emergencies if they have no experience of zero-gravity medical treatment. It is therefore highly desirable that future medical training should involve internship and training in space, possibly on the ISS.

Without taking into the consideration people's health outside the terrestrial sphere, humankind will never colonise or successfully establish itself in space. The important role of medicine in securing our space future is in need of serious review. ⌀

Previous page
Space hotel designed for low Earth Orbit by the Japanese Shimizu Corporation.

Opposite left
Kankoh-Maru spaceship
A fully reusable single-stage-to-orbit rocket, conceptually designed by the Transportation Research Committee of the Japanese Rocket Society. With prposed Shimizu Corporation space hotel in background.

Opposite right
Public entertainment area for sports, games and refreshments under micro-gravity. Picture courtesy Shimizu Corporation.

Above
Guest room module in space hotel. This area can be artificially maintained at 0.7 g for the comfort of tour participants.

The international design and consulting practice, Wimberly
Allison Tong & Goo (WAT&G), specialising in hospitality, leisure
and entertainment, has already acknowledged the potential
market in structures for space tourism. Here the company's
Vice President and Corporate Managing Director, Howard
Wolff, introduces the exclusive resort it has conceived
for those who want to get away from it all in 20 years time.

Space Resort

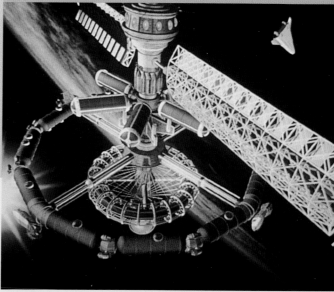

Wimberly Allison Tong & Goo has designed a space resort in low earth orbit utilising recycled external fuel tanks salvaged from future space shuttle launches. This proposal faced the WAT&G design team with a set of unique architectural challenges that were completely different from those posed by their normal work designing destination resorts. The intention was to develop an orbiting hotel in this new, vast and wonderful frontier, striking a balance between creating an out-of-this-world experience and providing some of the creature comforts that travellers have come to expect in other resorts.

The privately funded project is expected to be operating in the year 2017. The hotel will accommodate 100 guests as it orbits the Earth, 200 miles above the surface of our planet. Excursions will last between three to four days and one to two weeks (like a cruise). Passengers, who will be ordinary people, not superfit astronauts, will be ferried to and from the resort by the next generation of space shuttles or reusable launch vehicles that are currently under design.

The experience to which all passengers will be looking forward will be to share the magnificent view of the Earth from space. Buzz Aldrin, one of the first men on the Moon and advocator of space tourism, describes this experience as, 'like having a globe on your desk. It's a broadening experience after looking at parts of the Earth only on maps to then see them for real'. WAT&G's designers have enabled space-resort guests to do this through viewing panels fitted with computer-aided images to help them understand what they are looking at and to show additional relevant information such as local weather conditions.

Visitors may also have a chance to dock alongside, and pay an extraordinary visit to, the international space station (ISS), which will by then be orbiting the Earth; and for those with a sense of adventure, space walks will be possible.

The designers conceive the hotel as being divided between areas of zero and artificial gravity. This will allow guests to experience floating in space, and it will also provide a refuge for those passengers who may suffer from space sickness. An area with artificial gravity will also give guests an opportunity to partake in such earthly activities as taking a shower, or sitting down for a hydroponically grown meal.

The structure's design will resemble that of a bicycle wheel, which will spin slowly to create a percentage of Earth gravity at the perimeter through centrifugal force. Guest rooms and dining areas will be located here. The hub of the structure will house spaces for zero-gravity activities including sports and recreation and will also contain honeymoon suites.

Life safety is of critical importance. In addition to the issues one would deal with in a terrestrially based hotel, in space we need to be concerned with life-support systems, emergency evacuation procedures and protection from cosmic radiation.

Architects who wish to become involved with orbital design will acknowledge that this is the chance of a lifetime to create something truly new and exciting. To many, it will sound like science fiction. To architects with imagination and vision, however, it's not a question of whether, but rather when and how. ᴀᴅ

Opposite
The basic building module for WAT&G's space resort is the space shuttle's external fuel tank. Twelve of them will be linked in a ring, end-to-end, after being released in low-earth orbit from future launches.

Above
The next generation of reusable launch vehicles will transport passengers to WAT&G's space resort, which will provide partial-earth gravity in the perimeter guestrooms and weightless recreational activities at the hub.

Space Tourism

With the continuing expansion of the Internet, the future may lie in virtual rather than physical tourism. Anders Hansson, founding Director of the European Institute of Quantum Computing, asks whether we actually need to leave Earth to enjoy the spectacle of extraterrestrial tourism.

How can we bridge the void of space? In 1997, Pathfinder and its rover, Sojourner, used everyday photonics to provide panoramic images on television screens and Internet sites. The stereoimaging system on Pathfinder was developed by the University of Arizona, Lockheed Martin in Tustin and the Max Planck Institute for Aeronomy in Lindau, Germany. In general, it was based on the products commercially available over the last 15 years.

What will the situation be 15 years from now? By then, Internet connections may cover our solar system and many people on Earth could be controlling their own robots on different planets, from their homes. This would constitute only the first step in virtual tourism, where one could 'experience' the situation of the robot. Additionally, attempts are being made to introduce 'emotional states' into robots. A problem of scale remains, however. We know our scale on Earth, but how can we evaluate that on Jupiter? Such perceptual issues are much harder to solve than providing the information flow itself.

The systems described above, which present a combination of education and entertainment, are termed 'edutainment' and could turn out to be the biggest leisure activity of the 21st century. The World Tourism Organisation, a UN-backed organisation in Madrid, predicts that by 2020 tourism on Earth will have a turnover of more than $2,000 billion. And according to a *Financial Times* survey, 'Travel and tourism has not only developed rapidly over the past decades to stake a claim to being the world's biggest industry, it is, along with telecommunications and information technology, one of the fastest growing too.'[1] The fact that, 'even those holidays which were once the preserve of the wealthy, such as cruising and skiing, have been packaged and made affordable for great numbers of people', has increased the demand for yet more exotic experiences. An important problem for space exploration, however, is the lack of a mass consumer market, such as that for information systems.

It has been suggested by Bob Parkinson that through virtual tourism, 'we might map other worlds in the detail and range that we do for Earth – beyond any immediate hope of systematically analysing and correlating the data – at a cost far less than any human expedition'. Additionally, virtual tourists, 'could hardly contaminate the site with their litter or erode geographic features with their footprints'. According to Parkinson, 'Later, as with all tourist spots, there will be a need for guides and interpretation... The less adventurous, the less

informed, will need an explanation of what it is they are experiencing.'[2]

The final product has been described as follows: The year is 2020. You are standing on a platform at the edge of a thousand-foot cliff overlooking the Tharsis volcano on Mars. Your body casts a long shadow in the light of the setting sun as you scan the horizon for interesting features with your binoculars. Walking towards the edge of the precipice, you survey the texture of the rusty red boulders around you. Butterflies rise in your stomach as you peer over the cliff edge.
Sixteen hundred miles overhead, Phobos, one of the Martian moons, shines conspicuously. There is a new transport base under construction there. You move your telescope to get a better view when suddenly a doorway materialises out of empty space! A leg steps through. It's your spouse with dinner. Of course, you were never really on Mars. The 'platform' you were standing on was merely the floor of a small, comfortably furnished room called a teleporter. The walls and ceiling of this room are covered with one of the technological wonders of the 21st century: phased array optics.[3]

Polar-orbiting mapping satellites with quantum holographic storage and reconstruction can provide the technology for this new market.

At the age of 16, Albert Einstein imagined impossible configurations of electric fields in the physics of riding on a light beam; further developments crossed the light frontier into the territory of space-time in general relativity. In an article in the November 1979 issue of *Scientific American*, Bernard d'Espagnat discussed five out of seven experiments pointing in the direction of influences occurring at superluminal speeds. Two years later, H Lemke discussed the possibility of tachyon

Above
A night shot of the Rose Center for Earth and Space, showing the suspended sphere of the Hayden Planetarium in its glass cube. Through the Center's high-tech theatre shows and exhibits, visitors are already experiencing what it is like to travel through space.

Opposite
The Hubble telescope's deepest view of the universe.

Notes
1 'World Tourism', *Financial Times* Survey (City?), 18 June 1998.
2 B Parkinson, 'Shaping the flux – the Myth and the Future in Spaceflight', presented at the International Astronautical Federation Conference, 1997.
3 B Work, *Nanotechnology, Molecular Speculations on Global Abundance*, B Crandall (ed), MIT Press (Boston), 1996, p146.
4 H Lemke, 'Instantaneous Communication Over Cosmic Distances', JIBIS, 34, 1981, pp255–6.
5 A Aspect, 'Bell's inequality test: more ideal than ever', *Nature*, 398, March 1999, pp189–90.
6 T Ferris, *Interstellar Spaceflight: Can we Travel to Other Stars? The Future of Space Exploration*, Scientific American Presents (New York), 1999, p9.
7 Ibid, p91.

decay being a communication link.[4] In *The Quncunx of Time*, James Blish introduced the 'Dirac transmitter', where messengers are sent between such receivers, past, present and future. The Dirac transmitter should more accurately be called the Bell transmitter, since Bell's theorem states that any two particles that have once been in contact continue to influence each other until interaction, regardless of the distance to which they have moved apart. This was recently termed, 'one of the profound scientific discoveries of this century' by Alan Aspect.[5] Hence, there would be a faster-than-light communication network once the 'Dirac transmitters' had been located.

Timothy Ferris proposed in 1975 that interstellar civilisations would not travel but would instead use an automated network, 'deployed by small robotic probes ... each of which would set up antennae that connect it to the civilisations of nearby stars and to other network nodes ... each node would keep and distribute a record of the data handled. Those records would vastly enrich the network's value to every civilisation that uses it'.[6] As Einstein understood in 1935, two entangled quantum objects would immediately affect each other, regardless of distance, making quantum communication ideal as the base for an interstellar Internet. Einstein doubted that entanglement could be possible because of its nonlocal nature, but we are beginning to engineer it. The Ferris 'inconspicuous probes, designed to expand the network, quickly conduct research and seed infertile planets',[7] would have entangled pairs keeping contact with the sender's civilisation and quantum-based records, as well as quantum control instructions for molecules for life. Ferris's suggestion that we should look for information about extraterrestrial intelligence is a good one.

The question is: on which physical objects is the information encoded? Faster-than-light, hyperphotonic

Rose Center for Earth and Space
American Museum of Natural History
New York

Polshek Partnership Architects

The new Rose Center for Earth and Space, which opened in February 2000 at the American Museum of Natural History in New York, is allowing the public to take their first steps towards a journey into space, without ever having left the safety of the Earth! The Hayden Planetarium is the centrepiece of the museum's extension. An 87-foot sphere, which appears from the exterior to be floating in a 95-foot glass cube, it has a state-of-the-art space theatre in the top half of its interior. The space-shows transmitted in this auditorium use the most up-to-date virtual reality technology to give audiences the sensation of flying through the universe. Sources such as NASA's jet propulsion laboratories and the Hubble space telescope have been drawn on in order to dramatise the latest images and discoveries of planetary and space science.

Through the exhibits and the theatre in the Rose Center, people can experience the sights that missions, such as Beagle II, see as they approach Mars; and they will be able to venture further still, beyond the Earth's solar system, following the path of probes such as the space telescope to witness the birth of new stars andcontinue into the deepest reaches of the universe.

Above
Seating inside the new Hayden Planetarium.

Right
The Zeiss projector, which has been specially customised for the planetarium's unique space theatre.

Opposite
View inside the Lewis B and Dorothy Cullman Hall of the Universe, on the lower level of the Rose Center, during construction. Above is the sphere of the Hayden Planetarium.

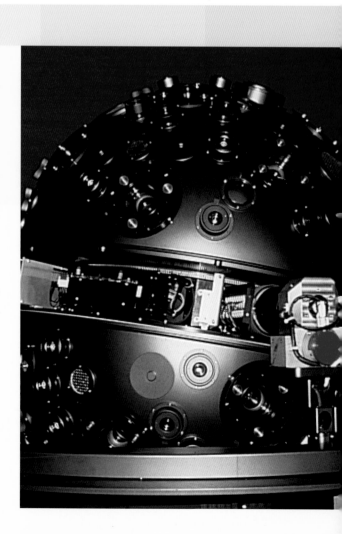

connections have also been called the 'cosmic glue'. To take one example, in 1997 Jakub Rembielinski, after a decade of investigations, claimed that at least 10 experiments on electron-neutrinos indicate a tachyonic-neutrino. Another example is the experiment with faster-than-light-photons.[8] The fact is, however, that we do not understand this glue, except that it takes place at the quantum level. Causality acts at the photon level and thus we will never see it being literally violated, but causality is an empirical observation: 'Quantum phenomena provide prima facie evidence that information gets around in ways that do not conform to classical ideas. Therefore the idea that information is transferred superluminally (faster than light) is a priori, not unreasonable.'[9] Aspect takes a different view: 'non-separability ... does not imply the possibility of faster-than-light communications'.[10] Hence, this is an open question

and, so far, only the photon knows whether a special frame exists.

Such an interstellar network would be the ultimate in surfing the Net. The issue is much more fundamental, since it is based on quantum control. What does this mean? One perspective of the change needed in our thinking is illustrated in a short story by Bill Johnson called 'Uncertainly Yours'.

The assumption is that we could double the effects of any quantum phenomenon by not observing it in detail, 'so when I started to measure the reactions and understood the system ... I collapsed the system'. Quantum physics describes a measured event as something very different from an unmeasured one.

Whether this is nature or our modelling is a big question. Another challenge is to grasp that while you read this sentence, the Earth is moving 300 kilometres in its orbit around the sun, the star itself is moving 2,500 km in the galaxy, and 600,000 kilometres of extra space is opening up for observation and virtual tourism. ᴆ

8 K Scharnhorst, Phys. Lett. B236, 1990, pp354-59.
9 H Stapp, 'Are Superluminal Connections Necessary?', 1977.
10 Aspect, op cit, p190.

Why go into Space?

With the 30th anniversary of the Apollo 11 landings behind us, the drive to explore extraterrestrial territories could be perceived to be waning. Or does the 1969 fascination with space still exist in the younger generation? Thomas 'T-square' Taylor, Ex-Chairman of the United Kingdom Students for the Exploration and Development of Space (UKSED) and his father, Richard Taylor a British Airways pilot who has seen most of the story of mankind's ventures into space unfold and has followed closely the development of reusable launch vehicles by the Rotary Rocket Company, consider their hopes and aspirations for space travel.

Famously, when George Mallory was asked during a money-raising lecture tour for his 1924 expedition why he wanted to climb Mount Everest, he replied quite simply, 'Because it's there'. In the same way, when we ask ourselves why we wish to leave the safety of the Earth to venture into space, we can conclude that it is human nature to be curious about the unknown. And although strange places may hold risks, there can also be huge unforeseen benefits. Until we go though, we will not know for sure.

Space is the greatest unknown, and perhaps the greatest adventure. It encapsulates the entire universe, including all that has been explored on Earth, and therefore encompasses everything that we strive for. The feeling that we can explore space, if only through bloody-minded determination, transcends the problems of everyday life. It is not an impossible feat and the exploration has already begun. Those who refuse to pay attention will simply be left behind. But

should we put human life and valuable resources at risk to achieve this uncertain goal?

Some say we need only send robots and the occasional scientist into space. This is a misunderstanding of the whole 'why?' question. The science is not the goal – it is a means to an end. The real purpose is to explore and live in these new places, to find out what they are really like. Man is the most adaptable and intelligent 'machine' we have; therefore, we should send people.

The current challenges are merely a step in human existence. It is not the fact that the area to be conquered is space that is important, but purely the idea of exploration. Were I alive when the Americas were being colonised, then I would have wanted to be part of that mission. But I am alive now, and the new frontier is the hazy edge of the Earth's atmosphere.

Only 30 years after the Moon landing, can anyone actually live in orbit? As a student on a four-year Master's course in physics at the University of Bristol, I have founded a branch of United Kingdom Students for the Exploration and Development of Space (UKSEDS) at the university, and held positions on the national committee for over two years. Through this, I have briefly seen behind the scenes of both the American and Russian space programmes. The cosmonauts on the Russian space station, Mir, stayed up there for three or more months at a time, working, resting and playing. That is longer than I spend at Bristol for each university term, and I consider myself to be living there.

This contrasts with the American astronauts, who briefly visit space on what seem to be 'business trips' during shuttle missions, gaining just a glimpse of what it is like to live in space. The different approach of the Russian cosmonauts has given them much more experience of how to live in space and partly explains why the Americans sought Russian involvement in the international space station (ISS). The disparity is also shown by the failure of many of the astronauts who visited Mir to deal with conditions aboard the station. The Russian view is perhaps more organic, more flexible. They used whatever they could to mend systems on the Mir space station, whereas astronauts may prefer to wait until the correct tool can be fabricated and sent up to them. Maybe this is why Mir had so many problems – things were never fixed completely – but it is also worth remembering that Mir is twice as old as its design life. It seems that while the Russians concentrate on living in space, the Americans focus on the science, and that this different attitude to exploring near-space has a direct impact on how we will use it in the future.

Would the Americans, with their philosophy, have kept one of their vehicles in use far beyond its design life, and would they have been able to keep it in good condition? During the shuttle–Mir missions, there were times when the Americans felt that the station was too dangerous and that it should be abandoned, yet the Russians stuck with it until August 1999. Two and a half years after its severe problems, it is still in orbit.

When thinking about how we will go forward from where we are today it may not be possible to state exactly what the far-off goals of space exploration are, because they will change with time, experience and technology. When we think about our reasons for going into the unknown and taking risks, we should consider the generations that will follow us. Perhaps the question of why we should go into space is no longer relevant: we should simply be acknowledging that we will. ⚏

At the time of the first moon landing, I had just started my professional life as a pilot and was glued to the flickering images that promised so much. I believed that by the time I retired, there would be a colony on the moon, maybe one at the L5 point in the earth-moon orbit, and an outside chance of one on Mars. What has happened?

Space has become essential to modern life. We depend on satellites for communication and entertainment. The aircraft I fly also use satellite, along with Global Positioning System navigation. But all this is inward looking: we have used space to make our lives easier and safer, but we have not exploited its full potential.

The aerospace companies have milked, first the government agencies, and now the commercial companies dependent on their unsatisfactory services. Rockets fail, yet companies are forced to pay the insurance because they have to get their satellites up there somehow. One of the problems is that the hardware is thrown away after one use, imagine what the costs of an airline ticket would be if the plane was abandoned after one flight. If President Kennedy had aimed, not 'to land a man on the Moon and bring him home safely', but to found a colony there, things might have been different. At the time, the X15 aircraft routinely went to space and back. If the money had been spent on developing these reusable machines, what would have happened?

It would have been realised that since it is expensive to take things up, but cheaper to bring them down, an Earth orbit space station should be constructed, followed by one in Moon orbit and in turn leading to the remote mining of the moon. This would provide the resources necessary, in more than sufficient quantities, at much lower cost, to begin to colonise space, and only then would men walk on the lunar surface. The cost might have been higher, but the saving in the long run would have more than compensated.

We cannot change history, but we can change the future if we wish. We no longer have the Cold War to galvanise governments into parting with the cash to invest in this, but the end-users of space technology – both investors and consumers – have an interest in bringing costs down.

It is not as if we have a permanent, inexhaustible supply of all that is required for the future of mankind on Earth. Industrial production should be moved to a place without an ecology to ruin, leaving the Earth to concentrate on agriculture. This would be a fitting project for the third millennium: to ensure the survival of mankind. ⚏

Opposite top
The UKSEDS Russia Trip at the Orevo Facility of Bauman Moscow State Technical University (Bauman MSTU) standing in front of an R-7 booster.

Opposite bottom
The full size model of the Mir core module in the hydrolaboratory neutral buoyancy facility at Star City (Zvezdny Gorodok).

Questions & Answers with
Buzz Aldrin

Most people can only imagine the experience and practicalities of travelling in space. Buzz Aldrin, now 70, was the first man after Neil Armstrong to set foot on the Moon on 20 July 1969 during the Apollo 11 flight. This is an edited extract from the National Space Society's series 'Ask An Astronaut', published on their on-line resource, which gave the public the opportunity to ask Aldrin space-related questions of their choice.

Some people believed that it was more important to feed the poor than send a man to the Moon. Having experienced the lunar environment, do you feel that the Apollo programme was worth the massive funding it received?

Yes, it certainly was. At the time, there was no greater goal, and our achievement has yet to be matched in any field of endeavour, in my opinion. Our efforts spurred a technological and educational push that has lead to incredible advancements. I believed then, as I do now, that our nation can afford to fulfil social as well as technical and educational leadership responsibilities.

I am 10 years old and would like to know what you were feeling when you were on the moon and said 'Beautiful! Beautiful! Magnificent desolation'.

Well, we were trained to be certain to make honest comments about what we were thinking as we made our spacewalk. I was thinking, 'We don't have much time here. I'd better make some sort of comment about what I'm seeing.' So I made that statement, and then went back to my prearranged duties. Neil and I were only out on the surface for two and a half hours, so our schedule was sort of packed.

How do you think the voyages to the Moon affected the different cultures of the world?

I think it can be said that the Apollo missions had a very positive effect on the world's population. The missions to the Moon provided a new perspective on our lives, giving each individual the ability to feel not only a member of a country or culture, but of an entire planet.

Do you think man is progressing, or just standing by watching as opportunity passes by? It often brings tears to my eyes to think that I will never see man walk on another distant body in my lifetime and to know that it was due to politics or lack of money.

Well, the history of humankind's efforts in science and technology shows many stops and starts. I believe that we must not allow our risk-averse media to create a society that becomes so cautious, so politically conservative, that we slow our exploratory nature from leaps, to steps, to a crawl.

Was there a point in either of your missions that you would classify the most:

a) scary? b) humorous? c) magnificent? d) exciting?

a) Everything is time-critical during powered descent for landing – computer alarms, longer than anticipated final descent, close to fuel exhaustion. Though not scared (remember, I was a Korean War fighter pilot), I was most aware that time was running out! Upon touchdown, I felt the opposite of scared: great relief engulfed us!

b) I made a crude attempt at humour by facetiously observing that I didn't want the hatch to close behind us after I exited the Eagle to join Neil on the lunar surface.

c) The accomplishment itself, the spontaneous observation that man had reached the lunar surface. I guess that people everywhere had the same feeling as we did. We made it!

d) It was exciting and challenging to say the least on my first Gemini mission when the radar failed intermittently and forced Jim Lovell and myself to compute the on-board solution manually to the initial intercept and subsequent mid-course corrections. That challenge was ironic because I had helped construct the procedures, which were based on my doctoral thesis.

I have done research on the variations in time perspectives of different individuals and cultures. I would think that normal biorhythms and circadian rhythms get severely disrupted when you have a personally disruptive launch schedule, a gruelling set of tasks to complete during the mission, combined with a context of constantly changing space, with multiple sunrises and sunsets in a normal earthbound day. How did the crew's time perspectives change during extended space flight?

On the Gemini and Apollo missions, we were on such a fixed schedule we had few, if any, thoughts about this. Our tasks were never 'gruelling', but they were certainly taxing. I found I was always in such a state of 'mission readiness' that I was not aware of the time of day on my watch.

The current astronaut crews, with many hours aboard the space shuttle and Mir, and in the future, the international space station, will have begun documenting the experience of unnatural rhythms. I would assume that they, too, will prepare for it and will become acclimatised to it. NASA, of course, has done vast amounts of research on this topic for space flight as well as aeronautical studies.

As a result of your Moon mission, what psychological, physiological and/or physical changes did you go through?

Physiologically and physically, I'd say that our Moon walk didn't change me at all. The intervening years have had more of an effect, as I age, than anything having to do with my flight experience!

Psychologically, my experience of dealing with a mid-life transition was difficult. I went from having reached the pinnacle in man's space exploration to having effectively nowhere to go – the Apollo programme was over and my flight days were done. I struggled with, and finally overcame, alcoholism and substance abuse, and now can say I've enjoyed more than 15 years in total sobriety.

How did you go to the bathroom during either of your missions?

With great care! Seriously, we used bags and hoses and personal wipes. The details are best left to the imagination, but there's really nothing gory in the reality. It's sort of like a long camping trip – you're glad to have a hot shower at the end.

With the recent announcement by John Glenn that he is returning to space, would you go back into space if given the chance?

I currently do not have a desire to fly on the space shuttle. Perhaps, when the next-generation spacecrafts are flying, I will apply for a ride.

Since government funding of future Moon and Mars projects will always be under attack by those who think the money could be spent elsewhere, do you believe it would be a good idea to privatise space programmes as much as possible – leading to more private space voyages by those of us who want to go?

Yes, I do believe that our government should privatise certain aspects of our space programme – by which I assume you mean the civil space activities funded by Congress and carried out primarily by NASA.

Congress should allow the space agency to turn over space transportation (shuttle), communications (TDRSS), and satellite manufacturing (other than experimental platforms) to private companies. Privatisation will eventually make it possible for average citizens to travel in space and will tremendously reduce the cost of all space-related activities.

Do you think that within the next, say, 30 years, we as consumers will be able to take a trip into space?

I believe it will be possible for someone to purchase a ride into space within the next 15 years. However, due to the current cost of space flight, I think it will be limited (at first) to the wealthy, unless we can devise some type of lottery to award flights.

Do you feel that the movie industry can be a catalyst in gaining the support for another 'giant leap' into manned space exploration?

Yes, the movie and entertainment industries could play a role in increasing public support for space exploration. However, for this to happen, the portrayal of space flight would need to be realistic and well supported by technically correct details.

Have you seen/do you believe in the existence of UFOS or other signs of intelligent extraterrestrial life?

I am generally sceptical of alleged observations of UFOS and alien visits. Yet in an overall sense, I feel optimistic in contemplating the probability of intelligence in the cosmos, hopefully nearby! I've written *Encounter with Tiber*[1] with this very idea in mind. ⚏

Notes
1 *Encounter with Tiber* by Buzz Aldrin, John Barnes. Paperback, 1996, New English Library, ISBN: 0340624515.

A novel set in the near future. The author has concocted a believable first-contact scenario and followed it through with an intelligent and often moving account of a human destiny entwined with that of another species. The convincing portrayal of the characters, both human and alien, makes the story so compelling.

Website
www.nss.org/askastro

Prize

Currently, a new space race is taking place between private companies and space enthusiasts to create the first commercial reusable spacecraft. Dr Peter H Diamandis, Chairman of the X PRIZE Foundation, explains just how important the $10 million X PRIZE could be to the future of space exploration.

A fact of nature is that competition drives success. Over the course of history we can look at events in every arena to support this idea.

Many of the most famous buildings in the world were constructed as a result of a winning design competition. The White House, the Eiffel Tower, the Sydney Opera House and the Gateway Arch in St Louis all began in this way. In 1792, $500 was offered for the best design for the White House, for example, and in 1948, a $40,000 prize was awarded to Eero Saarinen for his winning design for what is now the Gateway Arch in St Louis.

In 1419, the city of Florence faced what was thought to be an unsolvable problem – completing a dome for the Santa Maria del Fiore cathedral. A competition was organised by the city officials in the hope of finding a suitable solution. Filippo Brunelleschi developed a brilliant plan, constructing one of the most celebrated domes in the world and collecting the award. The X PRIZE Committee hopes that one of the 17 registered entrant teams will become the Brunelleschi of space travel within the next few years.

Today's $250 billion aviation industry began nearly a century ago with the help of incentive prizes. Between 1904 and 1930, hundreds of aviation prizes motivated entrepreneurs and aviators to design new aircraft that could fly faster, higher, more safely and cheaply. One of the most significant prizes of that time was the Orteig Prize, offered by hotel mogul Raymond Orteig, for the first person to fly between New York and Paris. Nine teams cumulatively spent more than $400,000 in pursuit of the $25,000 reward. By offering a prize instead of supporting one particular team or technology, Orteig automatically backed the winner, Charles Lindbergh.

The largest design competition to date is the $10 million award to the winner of the X PRIZE, the organisers of which are headquartered in St Louis, Missouri, home of Charles Lindbergh's famous *Spirit of St Louis* and Eero Saarinen's Gateway Arch. The $10 million prize will be awarded to the first person or team to build a reusable commercial rocket capable of carrying tourists to an altitude of 100 kilometres – to the edge of space – and of flying again within two weeks.

Competition also spurs creativity. Candidates in architectural design competitions are forced to use their imaginations and to think outside the box in order to earn the creative and unique distinction that will give them the edge on the

other entries. The same is true of the teams competing for the X PRIZE. Designs entered so far include an ocean-launched craft, vehicles that take off and land on conventional runways, spacecraft that land using a design similar to that of a helicopter, a vehicle that will launch from a hot-air balloon and a design that would be towed by larger aircraft before being released into the atmosphere.

Any one of these designs has the potential to open up space to civilians. Space flight is expensive mainly because there is not enough of it. There are only a handful of passenger-carrying space flights per year compared with hundreds of aircraft take-offs and landings per hour at the busiest airports. The way to lower the cost of space flight is to make it available to the general public. Rather than eight shuttle flights per year, there could be hundreds of tourism flights.

Recent surveys indicate that more than 60 per cent of the general public hopes to have the chance to fly in space and is willing to pay for the opportunity. The market for public space tourism exists; what we don't have are the vehicles to take us to space. Today, the only human-rated spacecraft are the US space shuttle and the Russian Soyuz. Both were developed under government contracts, cost a bundle to operate and have no chance of ever being cost-effective.

The 17 registered X PRIZE teams are from London, Moscow, Washington DC, Los Angeles, Houston, Buenos Aires and Denver, to name only a few. The entrants are currently designing, building and testing their vehicles. The X PRIZE competition will be the catalyst for the development of new low-cost spaceships. Some day soon, the next Charles Lindbergh, Eero Saarinen or Filippo Brunelleschi will win the $10 million X PRIZE. ⚐

Top right
Artist View of Pablo DeLeon's Gauchito during launch close to the Atlantic Ocean coast within 100 kilometres of Buenos Aires (Artwork of Martin Demonte).

Below right
The first stage of Burt Rutan's entry, Proteus, in flight in Mojave, CA.

Website
www.xprize.org

Moving in Several Directions at Once

Just as North America in the 17th and 18th centuries represented virgin territory for people who wanted to establish new communities free of ties to established society, space today poses the same challenge for groups such as the Association of Autonomous Astronauts (AAA). Here, Jason Skeet of the AAA explores the potential of space as a fresh territory and a means to take on government organisations.

A spectre is haunting the planet: the spectre of independent, community-based space travel. The Association of Autonomous Astronauts (AAA) is the most important space exploration programme active in the world today and, unlike other similar organisations, we have demonstrated the possibilities of well-planned assaults against the state, corporate and military monopoly of space exploration.

On 23 April 1996, we declared an information war against government-funded space agencies throughout the universe as the latest phase in our five-year plan for establishing a worldwide network of independent groups dedicated to building our own spaceships. We were therefore not surprised when, in August 1996, with the US government's announcement that it had possible evidence for life on Mars, NASA launched a counterattack against our space programme. This was carefully staged propaganda, designed to manipulate public support for an increase in the NASA budget. NASA want to spend billions on a trip to the red planet, asking, 'Is there life on Mars?' But for the AAA, space travel is an evolutionary process for the creation of autonomous communities in orbit.

In November 1997, as further retaliation against our independent space programme, the US military conducted tests with the mid-infrared advanced chemical laser (MIRACL), which has a beam about six feet wide to fire on an orbiting satellite in an attempt to destroy it. Predictably, the US government justified these tests, based at the White Sands missile range in southern New Mexico, by insisting that they need to maintain control over who has access to satellite information in times of war. However, we are convinced that the true motive was the threat posed to the state, corporate and military monopoly of space travel by the AAA.

After World War II, organisations like NASA emerged to regulate and control the developments in space exploration technology. Since the collapse of the Cold War myth, NASA has been desperately struggling for a new identity. The AAA has consistently opposed the rationale of government space programmes that regard the universe as a vast machine to be manipulated.

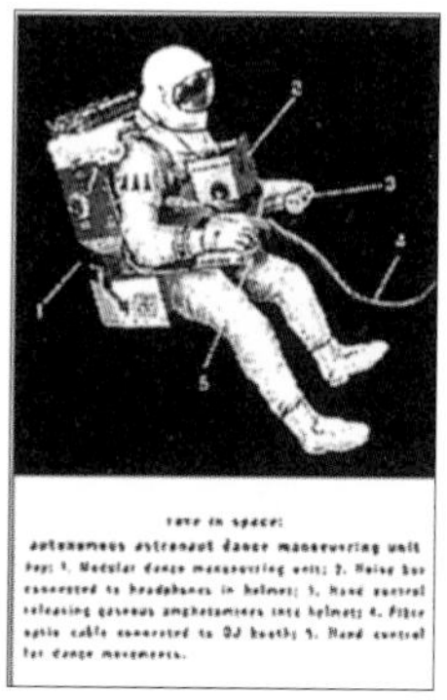

Above
Images provided by the AAA, illustrating their activities.

For example, we completely reject the idea of terraforming other planets as the action of an out-of-control capitalist system that has exhausted the Earth's resources and requires another planet to devour. (Terraforming is the creation of a potentially life-supporting atmosphere on a planet through the means of an outside force. This may come in the form of exploding nuclear weapons over the planet's surface or by causing a succession of meteorites to hit the planet. A massive 'greenhouse effect' is created, thus beginning the process that could lead to an atmosphere capable of supporting carbon-based life forms.)

The myth of space travel as the 'final frontier' (as propagated by government and commercial interests alike) is similar to that other myth about private space enterprise existing in a universal 'free market'. These myths are designed to mask the social forces that actually shape the present-day state, corporate and military monopoly of space travel. Plans to create a space-tourism industry confirm that the myth of the 'free market' will be projected into space in a bid to further fabricate the fantasy of capitalisms that are inescapable and omnipresent, like the force of gravity. We oppose these myths with our own specifically constructed and contradictory propaganda.

The various problems on the Russian space station Mir throughout 1997 have demystified space exploration for a great many people. Mir has been continuously patched together by its various crews, and this has enabled the technology to be thought about in a more down-to-earth way – comparable to how people relate to a second-hand car that needs constant attention. The events on Mir have also revealed the arrogance of government space agencies in allowing their astronauts to be so badly prepared for difficult situations. For example, when a computer failure on the space station led to a power shutdown that plunged the crew into cold and darkness for several hours, why had no one remembered to pack a torch with spare batteries, as well as several extra-thick jumpers? Anyone who has ever been camping back on planet Earth will know the importance of being prepared for these kind of emergencies.

In April 1997, the AAA launched the Dreamtime phase of the five-year plan. The Dreamtime is concerned with the possibilities that open up when we form autonomous communities in space, asking, 'What is the point of going into space only to replicate life on planet Earth?' AAA groups around the world are now exploring what kind of experimental modes of living can be created in space, what new social relations will be formed and what new activities will fill up the empty spaces that had previously fixed the limits of a complacent life back on planet Earth.

The AAA is concerned with investigating how a specific technology is used and who gets to use that technology. It is inevitable that the technology to build spaceships will become cheaper, and even that new technologies will be developed that will make present-day rocket-propulsion systems entirely redundant. But the AAA is the world's only space programme to make technological issues secondary to what we will be doing when we form autonomous communities in outer space. Our complex, interactive project completely changes existing notions of space travel.

AAA has understood that in outer space no one will be concerned with the compartmentalisation of knowledge into the particular categories developed by capitalist culture over the last 500 years. It is from this perspective that we regard the responses made by certain academics to the AAA's space programme, and in particular their accusations of an avant-guardist posturing lingering within the AAA's ranks. How can the AAA, as a worldwide network of local groups that simply aims to achieve space travel for everyone, be regarded as an elitist organisation? These so-called 'experts' fail to understand how the AAA regards history merely as a collection of fictions. Autonomous Astronauts pick-and-mix whatever contradictory and divergent ideas they wish to take with them on their various space travels.

In April 1998, the AAA launched the fourth phase of its five-year plan, described as the Consolidation, prior to the Final Push. Probably one of the most important observations to emerge from this phase is the experience of collective support and power, demonstrating that autonomous communities are already at hand. The fourth phase has also included rigorous training exercises that have enabled Autonomous Astronauts to remain completely imperturbable during the public presentation of AAA propaganda material. This skill is essential for expressing complex levels of meaning that can move in several directions at once, ideas that, for example, can travel from comical seriousness into serious comedy, a route that can foster further ambiguities.

Moving into the final phase of our five-year plan, it is our declared aim that all future discussions of space travel will understand how the AAA has revealed the contradictions created by the development of space exploration technologies. We are determined that space exploration will not be inextricably linked to the expansion of capitalism. We can go into space, not as conquerors of the universe, but as a collection of independent groups dedicated to building our own spaceships. ⨺

David Bowie

The public's backing of state-funded space missions and the future of space tourism is to some degree supported by the media's fascination with the extraterrestrial, which feeds into the popular imagination. Best known for his portrayal of space-bound characters is the celebrity rock musician and actor, David Bowie. Dr Rachel Armstrong investigates.

David Bowie was the first cultural icon to make popular the idea that space travel was possible for 'real people' by immortalising the doomed Major Tom in his journey into orbit.

This is Major Tom to Ground Control
I'm stepping through the door
And I'm floating in a most peculiar way
And the stars look very different today.
Lyrics from 'Major Tom', Space Oddity (1969)

Bowie's portrait of Major Tom became a metaphor for the human condition: faced with the prospect of no return, he wonders how we got here in the first place. He gives us a further glimpse of Major Tom more than 10 years later in his Scary Monsters album, where Major Tom finally jettisons all his connections to, and memories of, Earth by using hallucinogenic drugs.

Ashes to ashes, funk to funky
We know Major Tom's a junkie
Strung out in heaven's high
Hitting an all-time low.
Lyrics from 'Ashes to Ashes', Scary Monsters (1980)

Opposite and above
The Man Who Fell to Earth
(British Lion/BFI Stills), 1976.

If Major Tom is Bowie's metaphor for the quintessence of humanity, then his portrayal of Thomas Jerome Newton in the 1976 Nicolas Roeg film, *The Man Who Fell to Earth*, epitomises our precarious relationship with Earth and the fact that we take its resources for granted. Bowie's striking portrayal of the gaunt, orange-haired Newton captures the distress and despair of the Anthean who is trapped in human culture having left behind his barren planet where his wife and two children are dying of thirst. The alien becomes more isolated as he realises that powerful humans can be evil, brutal and corrupt, having little in common with the characters depicted on the American TV he had watched for years on his planet. His disaffection with Earth increases with time as he becomes more human. As his mission to build a spaceship to return home fails, Newton chooses to wallow in self-pity, dooming himself to life on Earth. The tragic story of *The Man Who Fell to Earth* illustrates the contrast between our potential to achieve great things as humans and what we actually accomplish on Earth, from the perspective of an outsider.

Bowie's repeated use of the theme of space travellers and aliens in his work draws attention to the quest for a united Earth culture that bonds people as a single race.

But if you pray all your sins are hooked upon the sky
Pray and the heathen lie will disappear
Prayers they hide the saddest view
(Believing the strangest things, loving the alien)
Lyrics from 'Loving The Alien', Tonight (1984)

In transcending our cultural differences by allying himself with 'alien' identities, Bowie suggests that unity between all nations can be achieved, and by looking out from, and back to, the Earth, he reaffirms our potential to achieve together the seemingly impossible. In characteristic style, Bowie has moved ahead with technology, updating this theme and phrasing the question in a new way.

Where do we go from here?
There's something in the sky
Shining in the light
Spinning and far away.
Lyrics from 'Looking for Satellites', Earthling (1997)

Bowie has successfully popularised outer-space through taking his audiences into new 'inner spaces' in his work that open our minds to the possibilities of a united human culture and the benefits of exploring otherworldly realms. ⌀

Fashioning

Space

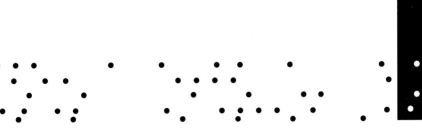

The demands of orbital life could lead to a new relationship between the self and the clothes we wear as exterior structures. Suzanne Lee, Senior Lecturer for the MA Fashion/Textiles programme at the University of Central England, Birmingham, looks at fashion's preoccupation with space since the 1960s and how, in the future, technology might become embedded in clothing and the body, eroding the boundaries between garment design and architecture.

Future life styles, where and how we will live and what we will look like, are central concerns for most fashion designers – the image-makers and trendsetters of tomorrow's world. Dealing as it generally does with fantasy, fashion is at the forefront of utopian visions.

Throughout the space race of the 1960s, Western designers celebrated the brave new world of space technology and futuristic architecture, often working with industry to create new man-made fabrics capable of sculpting revolutionary three-dimensional forms. The work of Pierre Cardin, André Courrèges, Paco Rabanne and Rudi Gernreich pioneered clothes for an egalitarian society. Cardin explains in the foreword to the book of his work:

Haute couture is a creative laboratory where forms and volumes can be studied. The immensity of the universe and the microscopy of the cell, computers and geometry: these are the sources of my inspiration. The garments I prefer are those I create for tomorrow's world.[1]

Indeed, Cardin counts walking in the spacesuit worn by Neil Armstrong on the Moon as one of the greatest moments in his life.

During the 1960s, there was still glamour in transatlantic flight, and the fashion designer's ability to sum up and reflect a cultural mood was harnessed by the commercial airline, Braniff, which commissioned Emilio Pucci to design uniforms for its air stewardesses. Pucci, who had himself flown planes in World War II, created a costume that incorporated a Plexiglass bubble helmet inspired by NASA astronauts.

On the 30th anniversary of the Moon landing, and with the advent of the new millennium, designers are once again looking to space for inspiration. At the couture shows in Paris for autumn/winter 99/00, Paco Rabanne showed a 'satellite' dress, while for ready-to-wear Helmut Lang produced silk 'space' suits; Hussein Chalayan's remote-controlled 'aeroplane' dress looked as if it could actually take flight.

Unfortunately, fashion frequently resorts to retro-styling, and the temptation to utilise silver and white to represent the dawn of a new age has become an unimaginative, futurist cliché. While it could be argued that the speed of delivery of fashion necessitates a high turnover of ideas, the absence of further development of those ideas appears to be more prevalent in the West. In stark contrast is the work of Issey Miyake in Japan, who for decades has worked outside the main fashion arena with the ultimate goal of devising a clothing system for all sizes and ages that is as easy to wear as jeans and a T-shirt (resulting in the much copied and globally successful Pleats Please range).

Fictional flights of fancy or facsimiles of astronaut attire do nothing to advance notions of dress on Earth or in outer space. For the most part, we are left with iconic symbolism as a superficial nod to surrounding developments in our culture.

More likely to consult the *New Scientist* than back issues of *Vogue*, Simon Thorogood is one contemporary designer who is predominantly engaged with the design and technological developments of today. While one can see evidence of a fascination with modern architecture and music, the dominant theme in his work is military flight, particularly Stealth and experimental aircraft.

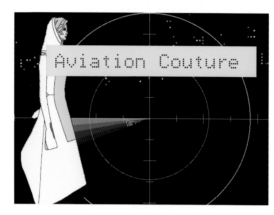

Digital Mode

As a member of digital art group Spore[2] and with a background in fashion, I was initially approached by Thorogood to work on the installation project White Noise[3] for his first couture collection back in February 1998. In an empty warehouse space at the Truman brewery in Brick Lane, London, he showed a series of seven outfits on mannequin dummies suspended from the ceiling and lit with a programmed

The inspiration behind the clothing was the result of a lengthy research project in which Thorogood applied stratagems from John Cage with the aethetics of early computer graphics and investigations into Stealth bomber technology

lighting sequence which added a kinetic quality to the static display. The inspiration behind the clothing was the result of a lengthy research project in which he applied stratagems from John Cage with the aesthetics of early computer graphics and investigations into Stealth bomber technology. The brief for the event was to create a context for fashion that challenged the traditional, I would argue outdated, catwalk and embrace a wider audience. The solution was a

digital space in which to site the hand-crafted clothes inspired by both cutting-edge and obsolete technology. Thorogood provided Spore with access to his sketchbooks, which revealed his working processes and which became the foundation for the installation.

My own research had already revealed an intrinsic link between textiles and computing, dating back to the 1840s when Charles Babbage witnessed the workings of the Jacquard loom in France and was greatly inspired by its use of punched cards to render woven images of infinite complexity in cloth. The binary operation of warp and weft led to breakthroughs in the design of his analytical engine, widely recognised as the mechanical precursor to the electronic computer. According to Sadie Plant in *Zeros and Ones*, 'Textiles themselves are very literally the software linings of all technology'.[4] We used the weaving analogy for the White Noise installation, along with the notion of 'Stealth' in graphics, applying the 'low observable' nature of the aircraft as a methodology for moving, concealing and revealing text and graphics within screen-based work.

The collaborative relationship between Thorogood and Spore has endured, with work exhibited in Denmark and Austria in 1999. We were invited to take part in *Fast Forward* at the Künstlerhaus in Vienna, an exhibition of the work of fashion designers (though with no clothes present) in alliance with artists from other areas, such as Comme des Garçons and Katerina Jebb. Spore's interactive digital runway played with the notion of the fashion catwalk – or 'runway', as it is often termed – airport runways and the navigational graphic surface they provide.

The catwalk was a 13-metre-long raised platform covered in pressure pads wired to a keyboard; decals on the runway surface hinted at the location of each sensor. Quite simply, as one walked along, visuals were triggered and simultaneously projected into the gallery space. By stepping, one could control the sequence and complexity of images, even changing colours within illustrated garments. The runway became an interface to the designer's clothing. Like a digital sketchbook, it not only revealed the garments, but also the research and inspiration behind the designer's vision. The public and press were therefore permitted access to elements of the design process that they would never normally witness.

Members of the consumer audience for fashion rarely resemble the catwalk model in size or shape, and it was this incongruity that we also hoped to highlight. By giving 'real' people the chance to take to the stage, regardless of gender, age or body shape, the usually passive role of the audience member is inverted and extended. On the digital runway you are both participant and spectator.

Fashion, particularly at the designer level, is a technophobic industry, suspicious of the creative potential technology can offer. It is within this domain that we feel interactive work has a role to play in making technology approachable, exposing the functionality and thus demystifying the tools. The exposed keyboard, with its wires and relays which click each time a key is depressed, makes visible and audible the connection of taking a step forward and changing the projected image. Thus, fun becomes a vehicle for the effective delivery of ideas. Immediacy and the ability to grasp what is occurring enable the communication of a volume of often unfamiliar concepts in a short space of time.

For the next project, Thorogood hopes to take this relationship to its logical conclusion, excluding real-life models and sample clothes entirely in exchange for a collection presented in virtual reality, constructed mathematically using algorithms and rendered virtually rather than sketched on paper and sewn in cloth. Clients would be able to adjust designs and play with colour combinations; a select-and-view function would provide instant visualisations, although the missing tactile sensation would still have to be offered by a real fabric selection.

Spore, along with many others, believes there exists a desire for the discrete absorption of technology into the fabric of our lives, to move away from the clunky, defunct hardware of screen/keyboard/mouse to a more intuitive experience. A future where technology can be embedded into our environment, clothing – even the body itself – provides a technical, intellectual and moral challenge to designers.

These are current terrestrial challenges, but what about when we leave Earth to inhabit space? Our insatiable appetite for new experiences and uncharted territories will undoubtedly mean we look beyond our world

for kicks in the future. As space becomes exploited commercially, the notion of space tourism suggests a myriad of opportunities for designers, architects and artists from all fields to ponder where and how our disciplines might be applied in the future.

Such a dynamic and exciting prospect as the design of a space hotel, for example, whilst a commercial venture, should be seized as an opportunity to push the limits of our knowledge, materials and skills – a chance to commission architects, artists, designers and musicians. (See *Future Systems'* design for a NASA space-station boardroom table.[5]) Research and development for space has always offered up inventions that have found their way into daily life (Teflon, Velcro, etc). This ongoing process of exchange between our terrestrial knowledge, informing design for space, and by-products from space research, enhancing the way we live on Earth, will surely also apply to the design of clothing.

Extraterrestrial Textiles

Rather than replicating terrestrial experience, building habitation in space provides us with an occasion to reconsider design for the way we live. It removes some obstacles found on Earth, such as commuting or pollution, and presents us with a new set, such as claustrophobia from lack of space and inability to escape. However, there is no reason to suspect that our values would change significantly, and thus we can assume that established patterns of social behaviour would remain constant.

The designers for outdoor performance-wear are arguably more akin to engineers than fashion designers, their concerns being to do with comfort, protection, movement, etc. Leisure time in outer space presents us with a similar set of criteria, where technology becomes much more integrated into clothing for performance, survival and safety. Emergent patterns in commerce suggest that as relationships are forged between industries, designers will increasingly benefit from specialist scientific knowledge. Chemists, geneticists, engineers and biologists all play a part in the development and production of modern fibres.

Current research into smart materials and sensory fabrics that can detect changes in body environment could be a valuable resource for monitoring physical and mental health on a space excursion. Conductive textiles will enable the integration of communication and data environments to clothing. This has implications for architects and furniture designers, since what we're ultimately talking about is a smart environment where one's body plugs into the clothing and the responsive space around it. Hence, the fashion designer of the future might be part software programmer, hardware engineer, architect, artist, biologist and tailor. ◬

Notes
1 *Pierre Cardin: Past, Present, Future*, Dirk Nishen Publishing Ltd (London), 1990.
2 Spore is a collective of six artists, designers and programmers united by an interest in digital technology and its place in shaping the environments in which we live and work.
3 The White Noise installation consisted of 40 vintage SE30s and Apple Macintosh Classics, machines dismissed by an insatiable digital industry as technojunk. We mobilised the slow processing speeds, low resolution and minimal memory to our advantage, each machine programmed in C to weave binary threads and random texts that cycle asynchronously.
4 Sadie Plant, *Zeroes and Ones: Digital Women and The New Technoculture*, Fourth Estate Ltd (London), 1997, p 61.
5 Martin Pawley, *Future Systems: The Story of Tomorrow*, Phaidon Press (London), 1993, p 84.

Space
Between

Inspired by Stealth bombers and X-planes, the
avant-garde couturier Simon Thorogood reveals
how his collaborations with far-sighted technologists
have changed the architecture of couture.

In almost every sphere of contemporary life organisations of all descriptions, from the arts to industry to science, have begun to adopt new strategies and ways of thinking in order to stimulate a fundamentally new space in which to conduct the future. This space will serve to entertain needs and scenarios that we didn't even know were there.

There doesn't seem to be much choice about this – the world is changing in so many ways that these alternative methods of doing things are often simply a strategy to survive economically. Small market players, for example, are assuming positions of trade that are harder for bigger businesses to imitate, and in the process are rewriting the rules of competition. In order for these individuals and organisations to find the future, they are having to observe and embrace ideas outside their own professional field of vision. Innovation will increasingly mean offering things in different ways and creating new combinations. One could say that the future will be customised.

Of course, within art and design there exists a well-documented history of interdisciplinary work and I would consider myself part of this, by now traditional, school. As a designer, I was drawn to the role that couture had historically enjoyed as the experimental wing of fashion. However, the notion of fashion as a cyclical re-examination of past styles or eras seemed totally without appeal or, indeed, future. The space between or around other subjects seemed a much more interesting and fertile place to be. I began to view fashion as the starting and finishing point for a form of cultural tourism.

I see this working practice as part of a bigger picture that identifies the role of the modern artist as that of an ideas curator. By creating personalised frameworks, a network of vaguely or clearly connected elements can be selected, organised and communicated. Transgenics, for example, the artificial transference of genetic material from one species to another, or the blurring of boundaries between animal, vegetable and mineral, was one comparative area that would have a significant bearing on my thinking. However, two subjects in particular were to prove especially stimulating and productive.

The first was music. Certain themes, approaches and composers continue to be tremendously influential within my work. In terms of the 'space between', I was intrigued by how much of this century's music has rejected absolutes: the beginning and end

of a piece, the distinction between composer and audience, sounds and their surroundings, documentation and so on. Music 'not going anywhere' has perhaps been one of the most important developments of 20th century composition, and as the Indian music of Raga illustrates, the space between notes has become the focus of much contemporary thought and activity.

The work of John Cage had a profound impact on my creative development. Composer, author and visual artist, Cage was arguably the most significant figure in the arts in the latter half of the 20th century, largely defining modern concepts of the avant-garde. Extremely prolific, he was famously known for his musical works employing alternative composition methods and for his use of the ancient Chinese oracle, the *I Ching* or Book of Changes. His prescribed use of chance has in fact been speculatively linked to recent findings in science concerning chaos and complex natural systems. Testament to his standing as a genuine innovator has been the extent of his influence on successive generations of artists, musicians, designers, poets and thinkers.

The lines and shapes of a composition could inform the seam lines of a jacket or the positioning of a placement print.

Alternative ways of scoring or 'suggesting' music, including those devised by Cage, had enormous conceptual appeal. These arrangements could take numerous and diverse forms: abstract symbols, numbers, textual pieces and colours. Not only were they visually pleasing, but they were usually tied in with a desire to free music from traditional or previous conventions. I looked to find ways in which to translate musical references into design strategies for garments. I began an extensive series of artworks directly informed by processes I had observed in my research. These pieces, involving text, colour, shape and composition provided me with visual material literally to build three-dimensional forms. The lines and shapes of a composition could inform the seam lines of a jacket or the positioning of a placement print.

The second major area of enquiry has been experimental spacecraft and Stealth aircraft. Stealth, or low observable technology, turned a completely new page in military hardware design. In aviation, it identified the blending of physical shape, new materials, radar cross section, infrared signature, performance, state-of-the-art avionics, thrust-vectoring capabilities, exhaust baffling, greatly reduced detectability – a whole range of criteria that significantly separated it from previous aircraft design.

In terms of aesthetics, Stealth has probably been the single most important theme in my work. Shapes and forms from Northrop's B-2 bomber, the YF-23 interceptor and a host of new-generation, unmanned combat aerial vehicles (UCAVS) have informed almost every aspect of my design process. The colour-blocking of military aircraft, in tones of grey with discreet and minimal blocks of bright identification panels, would provide the basis for the collection colour palette. The lines and panelling of part of the, or the whole, aircraft, often taken from specification drawings, would shape the seams, darting or silhouette of a garment. Text, symbols or insignia peppered around the fuselage, wing and tail (combined with graphic music scores), inspired the garment prints that would be quietly placed around the body. Stealth features, the concealment or baffling of an air-intake or exhaust outlet, would in turn define, falsify and distort sections of the clothes, around the face or hands for example.

The resultant garment was engineered not only conceptually but also in terms of its construction. A sleek, minimal silhouette was made up of various angled panels; shades of grey would be interspersed with slivers of bright inserts, and almost invisible prints would sometimes be located in unlikely places. Rather than using technofabrics, the collection was entirely made from pure silk duchesse satin, a traditional couture cloth. The duchesse had to be backed with three layers of silk and interfacings (not including lining) in order to achieve the required body and to facilitate the sharp corners of the body panelling.

Increasingly, and in line with my interest in Cage, I have become unhappy about having the final say in the design and presentation of my own work. As I had invested so much time and energy in the research and design of the clothing, I was attracted by the idea of working with another individual or group

In terms of aesthetics, Stealth has probably been the single most important theme in my work. Shapes and forms from Northrop's B-2 bomber, the YF-23 interceptor and a host of new-generation, unmanned combat aerial vehicles (UCAVS) have informed almost every aspect of my design process.

who could realise and 'finish' the work in media that I could not physically create myself. It seemed appropriate to show the garments in an installation environment where the visual and intellectual enquiries behind the collection could be made apparent.

This was to be the starting point of my association with the digital art group Spore, made up of artists and designers from various backgrounds who greatly appealed to my sense of cultural promiscuity. This interest in collaboration also extended to working with musicians, notably electronic collagists Barbed, and urban sound-sculptor Matthew Harden. The digital runway interactive installation, part of the *Fast Forward* exhibition held at the Künstlerhaus in Vienna (15 April–6 June 1999), was an opportunity for others to produce and arrange my work, albeit to a limited extent (see page 44).

We are now moving into a new era of space research and exploration. The US Congress has recently passed the Commercial Space Act allowing the private, that is non-governmental, exploitation of space. Investors, entrepreneurs and designers are furiously engaged in studies into more efficient and cheaper orbital space vehicles that will soon service orbiting space hotels. Thus the space tourist will be born.

As someone concerned with the nature of tomorrow's fashion, it is interesting for me to speculate on the look of the space traveller. I imagine the evolution of early spacewear to have certain parallels with the development of early flying clothes. However, it is probable that in terms of cut, fit and fabrication early space garments will be more akin to modern all-in-one flight suits or the two-piece shuttle suit.

A space trip could include official souvenirs and documentation, edited video footage of the journey, a certificate of travel and personalised space clothing. This last would have to fulfil various criteria. It would need to be comfortable, durable, yet easy to get on and off. Unlike the suits of earlier eras, which were tailored to each astronaut, the garments would come in a variety of sizes including widths and lengths of torso and different lengths of arms and sleeves. Shoes, of course, would be available in several sizes and would resemble a minimally but precisely designed trainer, either laced or Velcroed. In addition to the operator's insignia, the garments would be personalised with the traveller's name and coded tour details. This information might take the form of printed panels or removable tags, which could be read and processed by hand-held or fixed scanners.

During the outbound and return journeys, the garment would need to secure or hold any items required whilst negotiating zero gravity and would therefore incorporate a network of zipped, poppered or Velcroed pouch pockets, internally and externally. In the replicated gravity of the space hotel (created by spinning the station to create centrifugal force), where the traveller will have been issued hotel clothing with its own design and livery, there would be the need to keep certain effects on one's person at all times.

Although not intended as fashion, these garments would attain a status of extreme style and desirability. Exclusively issued to those embarking on space holidays, and as personalised and numbered pieces, they would very quickly become collector's items, attaining enormous cultural and historic value.

Initially, it is probable that the garments would be designed and manufactured by specialist companies catering specifically to the requirements of the space-tourism industry. Indeed, much technical information may come from space agencies like NASA, who have conducted extensive research on spacewear since the 1950s.

As the industry expands, the need to redesign and redevelop certain aspects will intensify. Clothing would be one avenue where new distinctions, levels or categories could be made apparent. This may lead to the development of insignia to show additional information about the voyage and traveller. Additional colours may be introduced, which again may reflect specific modifications and innovations.

Before too long, we may see a situation where prominent fashion designers are invited to design, revise or update spacewear for a particular operator or hotel – introducing a limited-edition cruise collection, for example. Just as there is an official calendar schedule for ready-to-wear and couture collections, a calendar might be established for spacewear collections. Rather than being catwalk shows, these presentations may utilise more contemporary means of presentation, perhaps even taking place in orbit itself. On-board scanning suites and design centres may ultimately allow the traveller to be measured and fitted with any garment they want from a particular space-range or designer collection.

Doubtless, a time will come when space tourism is as established as terrestrial tourism and the traveller will yearn for more and more individualism. In line with technological and aesthetic developments, space terminals, space vehicles, space hotels and space clothing will be increasingly modified and tailored to individual and/or group requirements and it is here that we might witness the beginning of space couture. The future customised. ∆

The Architecture of Extreme Environments

Designing for space, the most extreme of environments minus gravity requires architects to work without touchstones and with few prototypes. With this in mind, Ted Krueger, Director of Information Technology at the School of Architecture, the University of Arkansas, organised a design studio for his students with David Fitts, an architect with the Flight Crew Support Group at NASA.

One can consider extreme environments not in terms of their extraordinary uniqueness, but in relation to the commonplace, seeking correspondences rather than differentiation. The human organism has an envelope of viability that cannot be violated and therefore certain parameters must be maintained in order to support common activities such as working, eating, sleeping, socialising and so on. A useful approach is to examine the conditions found in an extreme environment and to use them to illuminate aspects of the commonplace that are masked by the conditions in which we typically find ourselves. The extreme allows for a new understanding of the common, and the insights gained are of immediate and widespread applicability to terrestrial environments.

The high degree of technical mediation that is required can be considered a precursor to the manner in which terrestrial environments, especially 'intelligent environments', may develop.

Within this approach, several aspects of the extreme will be examined. The high degree of technical mediation that is required can be considered a precursor to the manner in which terrestrial environments, especially 'intelligent environments', may develop. The experience of the low-gravity environments in earth-orbiting stations corresponds to certain aspects of virtual environments that are being constructed in the digital domain, particularly to issues of orientation and communication. Finally, it will be seen that the absence of a strong gravitational field allows for a reinterpretation of the social and cognitive utility of common objects. We will consider the correspondences between the common and the extreme and then present the results of the preliminary design exercise in the studio, 'The Architecture of Extreme Environments', offered to undergraduate architecture students at the University of Arkansas. Undertaken in collaboration with the NASA Flight Crew Support Group, the exercise was to design 'work surfaces' for microgravitational environments.[1]

Intelligent Environments

Extreme environments can only be made habitable by implementing technologies that mitigate the hostile physical conditions. Historically, exploration has extended the range of environments in which habitation is possible and has led to technical innovation. The aerospace and defence industries are currently developing a range of technologies that attempt to instill biological capabilities into synthetic material systems by integrating sensing actuation and control strategies into the structure of the craft.[2]

The objective of research into intelligent material systems and structures is commonly and explicitly biomimetic.[3] This approach seeks to duplicate the functioning of biological materials and living systems in synthetic artefacts. There is a growing recognition that the standard engineering practice of optimising the use of materials or systems of stable characteristics does not allow for the interdynamics that often occur in complex systems. In addition, designing for 'worst case' contingencies in an effort to accommodate the unforeseen (an obvious contradiction) results in inefficiencies in material, use and economy and limits the capacities of the systems in question. Biological systems cannot be understood as optimised in an engineering sense. There is neither an analytic decomposition of the problem domain nor a clear objective by which optimisation can be measured. Robustness of the kind found in natural systems is fundamentally at odds with optimisation. Biological systems exhibit autonomous, intelligent and adaptive behaviours. Techniques for producing these types of complex behaviours are developing in studies of artificial intelligence that consider embodied and situated synthetic organisms, in the study of autonomous agents and from within the dynamical perspective in cognitive science.

Having considered the trajectory of development in this research arena, I have previously argued that increasingly complex behaviours on the part of an agent cannot be met with brute-force programming.[4] The requirement that all possible states of interaction be anticipated and provided for sets a practical limit on what can be achieved. These limitations are simply a matter of mathematics. Repeatedly, as the combinatorial limitations become manifested, the designer is required to develop some means by which the agent can independently evaluate its context and take action. A measure of autonomy must be granted to the machine in order to be able to deal effectively with the complexity of its interactions with the environment – both physical and human. Autonomy is a fundamental change in the nature of the artefact which in turn requires a re-evaluation of roles that objects play in both the cultural and cognitive processes. It is this aspect of embedded intelligent

Notes
1 Dr Jerry Wall, Mary Comstock and the author served as studio critics. The studio gratefully acknowledges the time, energy and expertise of David Fitts of NASA and his staff. The design studio was funded in part by a grant from the Arkansas Space Grant Consortium. We would also like to thank the following people for their insight and assistance during the course of the studio: Dr Barry Brown, Dr Steven Batzer, Jerry Carr, Tim deNoble, Neil Garrioch, Dr Collis Geren, Dr Chaim Goodman-Strauss, Dr Ethel Goodstein, Ron Van Lammeren, Ilona Leonard, Pat Musick, Dr Bob Riggs and Kas Oosterhuis.
2 Ted Krueger, 'Like a Second Skin', in Neil Spiller (ed) 'Integrating Architecture', *Architectural Design*, October 1996, pp29–32.
3 R Measures, 'Smart Structures with Nerves of Glass', *Progress in Aerospace Science*, vol 26, 1989, pp289–351; M Gandhi and B Thompson, *Smart Materials and Structures*, Chapman and Hall (London), 1992; C Rogers, 'Intelligent Material Systems – The Dawn of a New Materials Age', *Journal of Intelligent Material Systems and Structures*, vol 4, January 1993, pp4–12; R Newnham, and G Ruschau, 'Electromechanical Properties of Smart Materials', *Journal of Intelligent Material Systems and Structures*, vol 4, July 1993, pp289–94.
4 Krueger, 'Intelligence and Autonomy', in *Convergence: Research Journal in New Media Technologies*, vol 5, no.1, Spring 1999, pp91–101.
5 G Pask, 'The Architectural Relevance of Cybernetics', *Architectural Design*, September 1969, pp494–6.
6 'Space Human Factors: Critical Research and Technology Definition', Life Sciences Division, Office of Life and Microgravity Sciences and Applications, NASA manuscript, 1996.
7 D Wolf, verbal presentation and discussion with students at the Johnson Space Center, 17 September 1999.
8 H Maturana and F Varela, *The Tree of Knowledge*, Shambahala (Boston), 1992.

systems that most profoundly alters our relationship to the products of our material culture. Gordon Pask posited that the domain of architectural design was not the determination of the form of the building but the structuring of the social context in which humans interacted with their environment and with each other.[5] He used the term 'mutualism' to designate a kind of symbiotic relationship between the architecture and its inhabitants. With the advent of autonomous systems, this symbiotic relationship acquires new saliency.

The technological systems that will be implemented in extreme environments will encompass a full range of intelligent media and material systems. According to NASA:

Future Space missions will employ extensive automation as well as extensive on-line resources. Automation systems may include rovers, robots, tele-operators of control, piloting and fault management systems. Information systems may include image, video and audio databases, medical databases, video monitoring systems, piloting systems, and electronic documentation for troubleshooting, repair, maintenance and training. Ensuring flexible intuitive safe interfaces to information and automation for both flight and ground crew is a fundamental challenge of Space Human Factors.[6]

While this list of technologies is extensive, few of its elements can be seen as exotic beyond the domain of their application. It is the pervasiveness and degree of integration that distinguishes them from those available in terrestrial contexts.

Habitation of extreme environments requires an insulation and isolation within a technical and wholly synthetic environment. It is the occupation of a technological apparatus – the inhabitation of a robot. As increasingly complex behaviours are implemented by means of autonomous technologies, the relationship of the occupants to their medium is no longer 'object to object' nor 'subject to object', but 'subject to subject'. The environment is no longer servant but becomes co-participant. This symbiotic relationship will accrue to common environments as well. In this sense, the highly mediated environments of extreme conditions function as test beds for developments that will occur on Earth.

Between the Physical and the Virtual
It is the absence of gravity that manifests the full extent of the body's conditioning in the gravitational field. Freed from this organising force, the body still finds a gravitational orientation bound into itself. It is bilaterally symmetric but highly differentiated along its longitudinal axis and optimised for opportunistic movements that are roughly perpendicular to the gravitational force. In the absence of technological developments, we are organisms bound inescapably to a surface. The implications of this inherent structure are difficult to ascertain when the only condition in which it can be apprehended is from within the field. Gravity is an assumption that could be relied upon along the full historical trajectory of the species in both its ontogeny and its phylogeny. Human experience of the absence or radical reduction of gravity has pointed to two broad ranges of implications – the physiological and the psychosocial.

Orbiting platforms have allowed for limited-duration experiments in the habitation of microgravity environments. The US Skylab and to a greater extent the Soviet/Russian Mir space station have provided the opportunity to study the effects of gravity reduction over a matter of months. Bone loss and muscle-tissue atrophy are two of the many pervasive physiological

---

In the absence of technological developments, we are organisms bound inescapably to a surface.

---

problems that develop during these missions and have resulted in the initiation of research programmes and on-orbit exercise regimens to mitigate these processes. It is clear that the body readily and swiftly adapts to the reduction in gravity and that the readaptation to the relatively higher stress of the gravitational field is a far greater problem. Dr David Wolf, the US astronaut who spent about four months on Mir, noted that even with several hours of exercise per day while in orbit, re-entry into gravity was a difficult process. Full recovery took about a year.[7]

On Earth the relationship between the body and the environment is dominated by gravity, which is tracked by both proprioceptive and vestibular sensing. The relationship between the sensations and the movements of the body allow for the understanding of the conditions that are inhabited. Humberto Maturana and Francisco Varela describe the organism as an essentially closed system that brings forth an understanding of both itself and of its media by means of a structural coupling with the media.[8] The covariance of the dynamics of sensor states in relation to the dynamics of effector states forms the foundation for this distinction. The drastic reduction of gravity removes much of this correlation and results in a kind of motion sickness, which is the result of the decoupling. The phenomenon is quite similar to simulator sickness experienced by pilots training on flight simulators. Once an adjustment to the absence of gravity has been made, a process that takes several weeks, the remaining sense of spatial organisation is dependent upon visual cues in relation to the body. While there is a strong tradition in Western thought that privileges an objective and verifiable physical world, we find that with radical changes to its environment, the organism retains a sense of its own coherency:

> It turns out that you carry with you your own body-oriented world, independent of anything else, in which up is over your head, down is below your feet, right is this way and left is that way; and you take this world around with you wherever you go.[9]

This is not to argue that a coherent orientation based on the axiality of the body is primary and inherent in the organism. These remain open empirical questions that are not addressed by the relatively short flights that have been made to date. It may be the legacy, the hysteresis, of the mutual specification of self and other that flows out of the structural conditions of the organism's ontogenesis. It is, however, understood to be an issue in the habitability of agravic environments. Astronauts encountering environments, information in the form of text or images and co-workers in nonstandard configurations have found the experience disorienting. Communication, a cultural condition formulated in gravitational space, becomes much more difficult. Legibility of time dependent on complex information, is hampered by these nonstandard orientations. While speech is the most malleable of the communication forms in this respect, subtlety in its interpretation is often dependent upon a variety of additional cues given by expression and gesture that are in themselves highly dependent upon orientation.

The absence of this normative physics is not limited to extraterrestrial conditions, however. The development of virtual environments holds out a similar condition. Issues of orientation within virtual environments is the subject of research into the ability to navigate and to work effectively in the digital realm as well. There is often a desire to impose an architectural trope on the virtual space as a means of organising and orienting the activities that take place there. This imposition effectively reintroduces a local

9 Henry Cooper, *A House in Space*, Holt Reinhart and Winston (New York), 1976, cited in J Schuster, *The Modern Explorer's Guide to Long Duration Isolation and Confinement: Lessons Learned from Space Analogue Experiences*, Anacapa Sciences, Inc (Santa Barbara, CA), 1995, p 146.

Issues of orientation within virtual environments is the subject of research into the ability to navigate and to work effectively in the digital realm as well

Top
Form and the resulting space are conditioned by the dynamics of the body. Design team: Sarah Broaddrick, Ladd Garey, Frank Graham, Sabine Krüger and Ron Ricker.

Bottom left
The international Space Station is organised as a three-dimensional rectangular lattice.

Bottom right
A portable and deployable surface may find use as furniture or as a spatial organiser. Design team: Clay McGill, Matt Galbraith, R Cary Blackwelder-Plair.

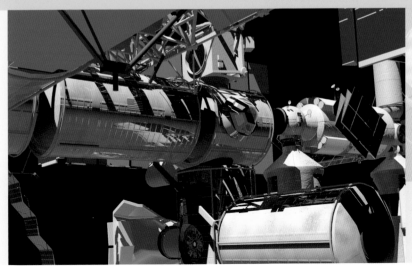

visual gravity and allows the body image to reinhabit a normative spatial continuum. The benefits of immediate and simple orientation are here exchanged for the potential benefits of exploiting the nongravitational virtual world. But understanding and providing for the need for orientation does not require the reassertion of global consistency. Devices that give provisional organisation to relevant aspects of the environment and its inhabitants may work just as effectively, while still allowing the freedom of movement to engender flexibility in the organisation of the environment at the larger scales. The correspondences between the agravic and the virtual suggest that designers for each type of space should become familiar with the experiments and experiences of the other.

The Cognitive and Social Dimensions of Environments

Extreme environments uncover hidden issues within common environments by reversing or removing constants or constraints that then allow latent variables to be manifested.

The relationship between the user or inhabitant and the environment needs to be carefully crafted. The view that design in some ways determines behaviour is far too simplistic and implies a pacification of the inhabitant that is unwarranted. The use of design as a tool of social engineering has been largely discredited. This behaviourist perspective must be replaced by an understanding of the relationship of an organism to its media that is informed by the biological characterisations developed by Varela. Here, the relationship between them is one of mutual influence and development.

Whether one sees the inhabitant or its environment as primary, it is the dialectical relationship that is faulty. Susan Oyama argues:

Amid all this shuttling between opposites, the organism is often reduced to an epiphenomenon – at best a battlefield where internal and external forces contend for causal primacy, or a patchwork, fashioned partly from the inside and partly from the outside. One gains little sense of an integrated and active organism from such presentations.[10]

Varela, Evan Thompson and Eleanor Rotch identify cognition with 'embodied action'.[11] In their view, cognitive capacity is rooted in the structures of biological embodiment, but are lived and experienced within the domain of consensual action and cultural history. Embodiment implies,

'first that cognition depends upon the kinds of experience that come from having a body with various sensori-motor capacities and second that these individual sensori-motor capacities are themselves embedded in a more encompassing biological, psychological and cultural context'. Cognition, then, is grounded in the organism's history of experience, in terms of its body and its social relations.'[12]

This reciprocal relationship between the agent and its media suggests that the isolation of cognitive processes as a phenomenon of the brain is an oversimplification. Kirsh and Maglio have shown that an agent's environment may be actively restructured in order to facilitate perceptual and cognitive tasks.[13] While clearly some actions in the world are undertaken in an effort to achieve functional or pragmatic goals, this work indicates that there is also much that is undertaken only to facilitate cognition or the pursuit of epistemic goals. Indeed, there are levels of complexity on which cognition can only occur by means of this structuring. Clark proposes that the concept of the mind be extended to include the environment in which cognitive operations are performed, based on the active role that the environment plays in driving these cognitive processes.[14]

The cognitive work required to land a plane takes place in part through the agency of the cockpit reference materials, markers and instrumentation that serve not only a recording or memory function but, by their configuration, allow for the instantaneous calculation and processing of certain critical information relative to the operation of the craft. Edwin Hutchins's analysis shows that the processing required takes place not within the individuals nor in the machine but by the agency of the sociotechnical system that they comprise.[15] It is concluded that the thinking that takes place during this activity resides in the hybrid condition of pilots and cockpit, not in one or the other. Here, the unit of analysis has shifted from individual components to the conjunction of humans and artefact together. This translation of perspective is of more fundamental interest and wider applicability than the navigational situation discussed. It suggests that much human activity and the artefacts that support it, at a wide variety of scales, are deeply implicated in cognition. This proposition also lends support to the symbiotic relationship that was suggested above. The pervasiveness of the cognitive role of common objects is not widely recognised. We tend to see objects as tools, as instruments of intention. We value them for what they can help us accomplish in a pragmatic sense. What this research suggests is that in many cases their most important role is to assist in our cognitive operations, either as individuals or as a collective. Hutchins suggests that cognition is the primary role of culture. It is within this perspective that the issue of agravic tables was addressed in the design studio. The absence of gravity and the questions it raises as well as the answers it engenders provided the students in the design studio with an opportunity to attempt to work directly with these issues.

Tables in Space

In developing a design studio that would take as its frame of reference the habitation of 'extreme' environments, we worked directly with David Fitts, an architect with the Flight Crew Support Group. It was decided that rather than selecting a speculative problem such as the design of a lunar base, we would work directly on issues that are of current and immediate interest to the development of the space station. The studio then functioned as a design-research laboratory considering a series of exercises throughout the course of a 16-week semester.

The problem posed to the students in the initial weeks of the studio was to make provision for 'work surfaces' to be used in the space station. This is not a 'toy' problem, but a real need that was recognised in the debriefing sessions following previous flights of the space shuttle and the experiences of long-duration missions on Mir and Skylab. The lack of these surfaces on prior missions was due to some extent to the fact that they are not needed from the standpoint of pragmatic functions relative to the task at hand. Initially, this seems a simplistic and wholly pragmatic operation. Yet the nature of the table without gravity has had little investigation. The 'default setting' – a rectangle on four legs – has no meaning or utility in this context. Without gravity, there is no need to support the work on a table. Nevertheless, the crew regularly asked to have some kind of working surface. Those proposed in this studio are intended to be used as needed during the full range of activities undertaken by astronauts. This may include conducting, managing and recording the progress of scientific experiments, maintaining the craft and the astronaut and communicating. These requirements imply adaptability to a wide range of conditions and functions over the projected 30-year utility of the station. This long-range time frame also indicated that the incorporation of current computer technology as a portable information-processing machine, initially a popular

proposition in the studio, would be of short-lived utility. The tables, therefore, sought to define relatively basic and stable issues. The cognitive and social uses of inhabited spaces soon surfaced.

Kirsh examined the use of space as a means to organise and track activities, to calculate and to sequence work.[16] Space in these cases is an active medium of cognitive organisation and processing external to the agent. Kirsh uses as examples the preparation of food. There is a level of correspondence between a kitchen and a laboratory that most designers will immediately recognise is borne out in their forms. Clearly, the general needs for instructions, preparation, organisation and execution of the tasks is quite similar. One of the primary uses of the microgravity work surfaces is to provide the infrastructure that facilitates this cognitive organisation in a manner that is integrated into the activities taking place. The reduction of functional requirements due to the absence of gravity allows the epistemic requirements to become prominent.

One aspect basic to cognitive organisation is the separation of the activity at hand from the surroundings. The absence of gravity suggests that vertical or developed surfaces can have the utility accorded horizontal surfaces on Earth and, in addition, serve to define a 'zone of work'. The space station is an assembly of canister-like modules organised into a Cartesian lattice by means of connecting nodes. The spatial implication of this strategy is that the interior is a continuum of corridor spaces lined by storage, support and equipment racks. Most of the space is simple, tubular and immediately apprehended. The kind of separation required for concentrated work or personal privacy is difficult to obtain unless one has an entire module to oneself. This luxury can rarely be counted upon. Several schemes developed that could address this issue. One uses as its point of departure the geometry of the arm.[17] In the absence of gravity, the arms tend to float up and there is no additional effort required in the reach. A curved surface makes all the activity equidistant. There is no need to reach over some of the work to access the remainder. The resulting surface can be oriented to act as a screen to surrounding activity. The 'chair' portion of this scheme is composed of spring steel and moulded rubber. It provides a flexible framework against which the astronaut can exert pressure. This provides a means of exercise while seated at a task. Another project conceives of the table as a 'deployable surface' that expands to span the typical interior width.[18] This gives some flexibility in the locations in which it can be installed and temporarily allows the work surface to define relatively more isolated areas within a module that may, for example, be used as sleeping or working areas.

10 S Oyama, 'Does Phylogeny Recapitulate Ontogeny?', in F Varela and JP Dupuy, *Understanding Origins, Contemporary Views on the Origin of Life, Mind and Society*, Boston Studies in the Philosophy of Science, vol 130, Klewer Academic Publishers (Dordrecht, NL), 1992, pp 227–232.
11 Varela, E Thompson and E Rotch, *Embodied Mind*, MIT Press (Cambridge, MA), 1991.
12 Varela, 'Whence Perceptual Meaning? A Cartography of Current Ideas', in Varela and Dupuy, *Understanding Origins*, op cit, pp 235–263.
13 D Kirsh and P Maglio, 'On distinguishing Epistemic from Pragmatic Activity', *Cognitive Science* 18(4), 1994, pp 513–549.
14 A Clark, *Being There: Putting Brain, Body and World Back Together Again*, MIT Press (Cambridge, MA), 1997.
15 E Hutchins, 'How a Cockpit Remembers Its Speeds', *Cognitive Science*, 19, 1995, pp 265–288.
16 D Kirsh, 'The Intelligent Use of Space', *Artificial Intelligence*, 73 (1–2), 1995, pp 1–30.
17 Team members: Sarah Broaddrick, Ladd Garey, Frank Graham, Sabine Krüger, Ron Ricker.
18 Team members: Clay McGill, Matt Galbraith, R Cary Blackwelder-Plair.

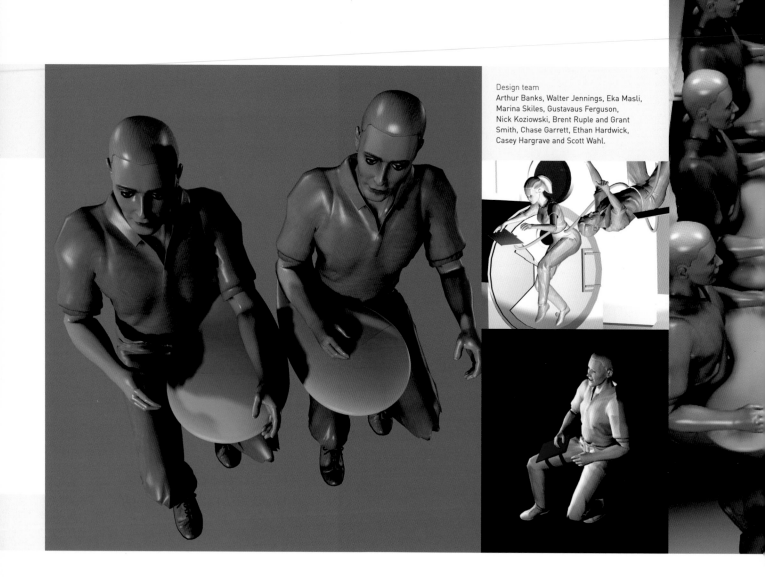

Design team
Arthur Banks, Walter Jennings, Eka Masli,
Marina Skiles, Gustavaus Ferguson,
Nick Koziowski, Brent Ruple and Grant
Smith, Chase Garrett, Ethan Hardwick,
Casey Hargrave and Scott Wahl.

Above left
The geometry of the table
is generated by the space
requirements of social
interaction.

Above top right
Astronauts, worksurfaces
and the space craft are united
and organised by a flexible
infrastructure of ultilities
and communications.

Above bottom right
The requirements for
convenience and mobility
and the lack of weight
results in a wearable furniture.

Centre image
The concatination of many
individual tables produces
a surface of common
orientation for the floating
astronauts.

The individual use of tables in this environment implies that they be mobile but fixable to the craft, or alternatively to the astronaut, as a kind of wearable furniture. It will be seen that several teams developed designs that can be fixed to the individual astronaut. As these surfaces would be used for a variety of tasks, some flexibility in their configuration is desirable. One team developed a scheme that would make use of a semirigid connecting link between either the craft or the user.[19] This link allows for an infinite variety of adjustments between the user and the surface. Multiple, quick-connect couplings on a belt would allow astronauts to fix themselves to a point in the station as well, by means of a second link. This connection could support the provision of a number of utilities – water, power and communications – on to the work surface. Task lighting becomes a possibility that does

not presently exist. Chains of users and tables would create a local network of utilities and communications that could support collaborative work.

The surfaces need to be able not only to support collaborative work in small groups, but to combine into configurations that support the simultaneous activity of the whole crew, a population of seven, for meals, planning, conferences and briefings. The table's role in these cases may incorporate the cognitive functions discussed and in addition serve to organise and articulate a variety of social relationships.

Another team developed a scheme that was based on the interface between the surface and the body.[20] The 'kidney' allowed for the use of the table as a centre of activity as well as providing a staging area off to the side. An important aspect of this table is the development of its curved outer surface. The interface between two or more of these cam-like curves produced a continuously varying geometry that is able to accommodate a variety of interpersonal situations.

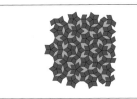

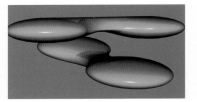

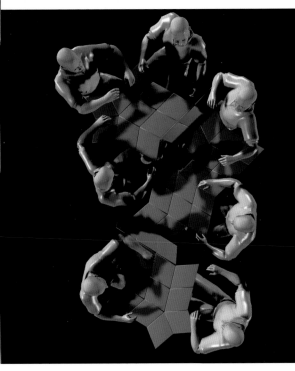

The side-by-side collaborative mode allows for closer spacing between individuals when attention is towards an external object or situation. Face-to-face direct communication is afforded more distance. The ability continuously and dynamically to reconfigure the spatial relationships engendered by the surfaces in response to changes in the social dynamics of the activity or conversations may be critical to the maintenance of interpersonal relationships. This has particular significance in the context of a small, multicultural isolated group on long-duration missions. In this project, aspects of the environment are developed in order to allow for, rather than to proscribe or attempt to determine, the behaviour of the inhabitants.

A further development resulted in a simple unit composed of two circular lobes joined by a concave midsection. The shape of these tables allows for a variety of positions relative to the body and a variable geometry relative to additional adjacent units, enabling configurations suitable for many different uses. The sectional geometry of the centre portion of the 'bongo table' has been developed so that, when inverted and locked together, two units form the nucleus of further configurations. A wide range of configurations can be developed from this simple 'primitive'.

An alternative approach to the problem of grouping individual units into larger configurations is to consider them instances of tiling, of shapes that fill surfaces. The aperiodic Penrose tiling is perhaps the best-known example. The team implemented one of its members, a rhombus with angles of 72 and 108 degrees.[21] The more acute shape shown in the Penrose tiles was considered too limited in its utility. These simple, identical modules are capable of combining into a wide variety of composite shapes. They can fill a plane, of course, but can also be configured into three-dimensional surfaces. The resulting spaces are suitable for privacy and

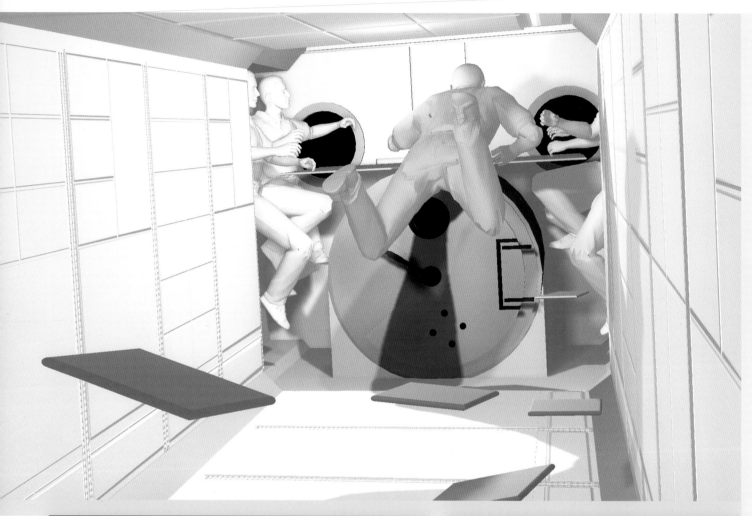

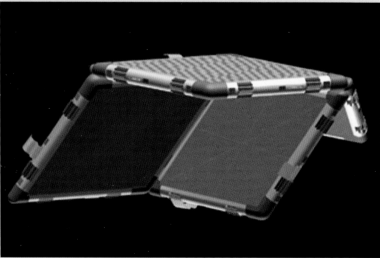

Top
Rhombics flock about the craft as a species of autonomous roving furniture.

Centre left
The rhombic geometry is capable of configurations that have inherent structural capacities.

Centre right
These simple units have the ability to become developed surfaces with spatial implications.

Bottom right
The Personal Satellite Assistant is an autonomous and intelligent object currently under development at NASA.

Design team
Arthur Banks, Walter Jennings, Eka Masli and Marina Skiles.

concentration. Both the 'rhomboid' and 'bongo' schemes use the geometric properties of the objects as physical instantiations of simple-rule systems that are capable of developing into more complex configurations.

While the tables have a series of defined functions, they may also integrate others. There is a tendency for objects to leave surfaces

It has been found that the lack of convective currents in microgravity causes a build-up of carbon dioxide in the vicinity of workers stationary for a long period of time. This affects wakefulness and concentration.

when there is no force to hold them in place. A solution was discovered on Mir. The cosmonauts covered a return air duct with a permeable fabric and used the suction produced to fix small objects in place. Work surfaces integrated with this capability would have additional benefits as well. It has been found that the lack of convective currents in microgravity causes a build-up of carbon dioxide in the vicinity of workers stationary for a long period of time. This affects wakefulness and concentration. A similar problem occurs with temperature, as heat does not rise but forms a zone around its source. The mixing of air in proximity to the table by means of embedded fans would be beneficial in both cases.

Integrated fans may also provide the tables with a motive force and directional control by means of the fans' exhausts. Movement throughout the station would allow for a secondary function when the work surfaces are not directly employed by the astronauts. The 'flocking rhomboids' are an autonomous

species of roving furniture that use the air movements through the table surface as a filter to clean the air of a variety of particles that would simply fall to earth in terrestrial environments. In microgravity, their continuous circulation poses vexing problems for both equipment operation and occupant comfort. The tables would return to a base station for cleaning and recharging. In order to flock and navigate, and to avoid harassing the humans, the rhomboids would be equipped with a suite of sensors and behavioural algorithms. None of these are beyond the capabilities of current robotic technology. There is, in fact, a NASA project presently in prototype that uses just such technologies.[22] The personal satellite assistant is intended to be deployed within the station. One of its projected uses is as an artificially intelligent assistant running an 'expert system' and knowledgeable about experiments being flown on the station. Its task would be to monitor experiments and advise the astronauts, troubleshooting problems that arise with the project. A prototype autonomous eye, an extravehicular camera, has already been tested in the cargo bay of the space shuttle.[23] Marcel Schoppers describes an earlier proposal for an autonomous extravehicular robot to retrieve tools and perhaps personnel that drift from the exterior of the craft.[24] In each of these proposals, the autonomy of the object is a means to reliability, reduced risk and flexibility.

One aspect of many of the schemes presented here is the use of the table as a local common plane of reference relative to interpersonal orientation. It is critical in a potentially high-stress, multicultural environment that the clarity of communication be maintained. The provision of an organising surface that operates in the cognitive as well as in the social realm provides the physical infrastructure for collaborative work. The table is then a catalytic surface that allows interactions to precipitate under suitable conditions.

It has been argued that a consideration of extreme conditions can shed new light on aspects of the commonplace. This is not to deny the uniqueness of the extreme, but to show that the common might best be understood when an alternative is present – a sample population of one may not be particularly informative. The correspondences between the highly technical environments engendered by extreme conditions and the intelligent environments that we are in the process of creating, and the relationship between agravic and virtual environments and the cognitive and social utility of common objects have served to illustrate this thesis. It is not only technology that can be transferred from the exploration of space. Also of value is the perspective shift that develops from consideration of the alteration to the context in which we understand ourselves. △D

19 Team members: Chase Garrett, Ethan Hardwick, Casey Hargrave, Scott Wahl.
20 Team members: Gustav aus Ferguson, Nick Kozlowski, Brent Ruple, Grant Smith.
21 Team members: Arthur Banks, Walter Jennings, Eka Masli, Marina Skiles.
22 See: www.arc.nasa.gov/ic/psa/
23 See: http://tommy.jsc.nasa.gov/proj ects/Sprint/aercam-sprint-overview.html; and http://spaceflight.nasa.gov/stat ion/assembly/sprint
24 M Schoppers, 'The Use of Dynamics in an Intelligent Controller for a Space Faring Robot', in P Agre and S Rosenschein (eds), *Computational Theories of Interaction and Agency*, MIT Press (Cambridge, MA), 1996, pp 541–596.

Robert T McCall, *Argosy*. This gravity free entity-city-resort of the future hovers above the landscape.

New
Horizons

Robert T McCall, *The Prologue and the Promise*. This detail from a large mural depicts the evolution of world civilisation.

Official artist to NASA, Robert T McCall has visually documented the space programme for more than 35 years. Having followed the progress of how humankind may exist beyond the Earth's atmosphere at first hand, he has been employed as a conceptual artist on major movies such as Stanley Kubrick's *2001: A Space Odyssey* (1968), the Star Trek movies and Disney's *The Black Hole* (1979).

Aaah ...

Quantum City

... Aaahyaah ...

Architect Mathis Osterhage's 'Quantum City' uses a comic-strip format to explore the possibilities of long-term urban settlement in space. His designs defy the laws of physics as we presently understand them on Earth.

... Aaah ...

Alright ?

... Aaahyaah ...

Ha ha ha, Lets go!

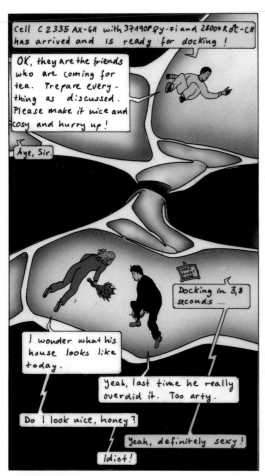

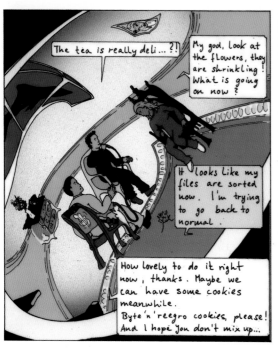

On the Possibility of

Terraforming Mars

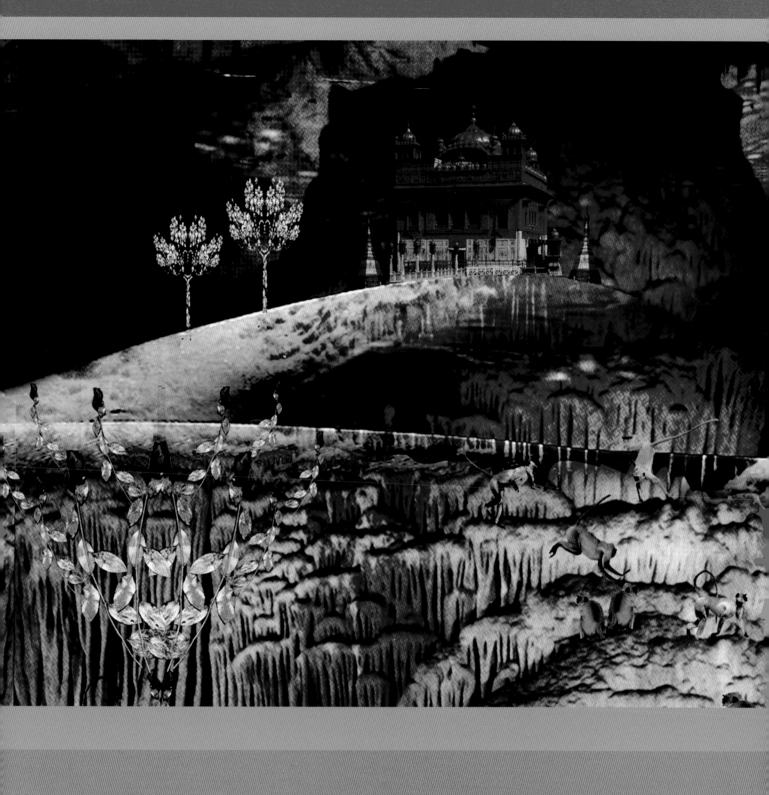

As humans cannot yet inhabit the native surface of a planet such as Mars, they must change its local conditions in order to sustain life there. Martyn J Fogg, science writer and internationally recognised researcher on the subject of terraforming, discusses how this might be achieved.

Introduction

If space exploration can be said to have a purpose beyond that of reconnaissance and understanding of the universe, it is expressed by many involved in the space business as 'space settlement': the founding of new branches of civilisation remote from the Earth.[1] However, the technical issues involved in a permanent stay remote from our salubrious home-world are far from trivial. Initial missions such as visits to other planets, followed by outposts and pioneering settlements, are all likely to have their life-support subsidised in the form of machinery and consumables supplied from Earth. This strategy will not be sustainable for long. To achieve growth and permanency, space-based civilisations must harness local resources in autonomous and stable bioregenerative life-support systems, energised by the sun.

Contemplation of this problem is divided between the study of the settlement of planetary surfaces and of interplanetary space. The latter involves the fabrication of large, orbiting habitats with landscaped interiors, which must import, contain and recycle all their bioconsumables.[2] Any contained and miniaturised biosphere such as this must inevitably submit to some mechanical involvement in life-support, in addition to keeping at bay the lethal vacuum outside. Colonising a planetary surface, especially one such as Mars, where all the chemical requirements of life are to be found, has the advantage of local resources. However, enclosed colonies on planetary surfaces are, in essence, little different from grounded spacecraft in that they must still resist, rather than incorporate, the surrounding environment. This strategy discounts the habitable potential of a planet such as Mars, which, due to its gravity well, is inherently capable of hosting a global, uncontained biosphere similar to that of the Earth.[3] Since the biosphere of the Earth is the one known life-support system capable of self-maintenance over an indefinite period, it follows that the ultimate strategy involved in space settlement will be to create counterpart Earths elsewhere, by engineering sterile planets to life. This hypothetical process is known as 'terraforming', a word originally coined in science fiction,[4] now adopted by science and, lately, officially admitted into the English language.[5] It can be defined as a process of planetary engineering, specifically directed at enhancing the capacity of an extraterrestrial planetary environment to support life. The ultimate in terraforming would be to create an uncontained planetary biosphere emulating all the functions of the biosphere of the Earth – one that would be fully habitable for human beings.[6]

Ecopoiesis

Assuming Mars is indeed a barren planet, any terraforming process is likely to take it on a path from sterility through a continuum of improving habitable states. 'Full' terraforming though (the creation of an aerobic biosphere suitable for humans and other animals), is likely to remain a distant, although not impossible, goal. Fortunately, however, significant advantages for human habitation will accrue well before full habitability is attained. A denser atmosphere will provide better shielding from cosmic rays, facilitate aerobraking and flight, and would permit the construction of ambient pressure habitats and

the replacement of pressure suits with simple breathing gear. Exterior atmospheric, hydrological and biogeochemical cycles could be exploited as sources of power and food.

The first biological step in a terraforming process is known as 'ecopoiesis', a term invented by Robert Haynes in 1990, from the Greek roots *oikos*, an abode, house or dwelling place, and *poiesis*, a fabrication or production. It has been defined as, 'the fabrication of an uncontained, anaerobic, biosphere on the surface of a sterile planet. As such, it can represent an end in itself or be the initial stage in a more lengthy process of terraforming.'[7] Unfortunately, ecopoiesis cannot be accomplished right away and without preparation, as no known biota can simply be scattered on the Martian surface and expected to thrive. A degree of environmental modification will be required to create the conditions needed for even the hardiest of extremophiles (such as Antarctic cyanobacteria and lichens) to take on Mars as their new home. This initial planetary engineering, leading to ecopoiesis, has been the focus of most terraforming-related research.

In order for ecopoiesis to be possible, four principal modifications must be applied to the Martian environment:

1 The mean global surface temperature must be increased by ~ 60 kelvin,
2 The mass of the atmosphere must be increased,
3 Liquid water must be made available,
4 The surface ultraviolet and cosmic ray flux must be substantially reduced.

These environmental changes would be sufficient to render Mars habitable for certain anaerobic ecosystems, but not, as is often stated, for plant life. An additional requirement for plants is the presence of sufficient atmospheric oxygen to allow for root respiration,[8] and although this would be much less than that needed for animals to breathe (perhaps as low as $pO_2 = 20$ millibars), such a quantity of oxygen is not expected to be released during initial planetary engineering. Thus, a fifth environmental modification will be needed for further terraforming:

5 The atmospheric composition must be altered to increase its oxygen and nitrogen fractions.

It is simple to list such requirements, but less easy to imagine engineering them on a planetary scale. However, there are two mitigating features. The first is that all these modifications are related, so that effecting one also causes the others to move in the desired direction. For instance, an increase in the mass of the atmosphere improves its function as a meteor and radiation shield; enhances the greenhouse effect (thus increasing surface temperature); and widens the stability field of liquid water. The second mitigating feature is the possibility of exploiting positive feedback processes intrinsic to the Martian climate system that will serve to amplify any engineered climatic forcing. This would mean that not every additional kilogram of atmosphere, or every degree of temperature rise, would have to be directly 'manufactured' by planetary engineers; instead, a comparatively small forcing could push Mars over an environmental cusp catastrophe, whereupon its climate is spontaneously drawn towards a quasi-stable high-temperature regime.

The Runaway CO_2 Greenhouse

It is often noted that the oldest surfaces of Mars are marked by numerous river-cut features, suggesting that the planet was once warmer and possessed a much denser atmosphere, predominantly composed of carbon dioxide.[9]

Ecopoiesis models of the climatic-feedback-type are inspired by the notion of re-creating this archaic 'warm and wet' Mars. The principal assumptions of these models are that much of this CO_2 is still present on Mars in a labile form accessible to planetary engineers. It is proposed that an initial engineered warming of Mars, which need not be very extensive, will cause some CO_2 to enter the atmosphere from surface reservoirs. This will augment the atmospheric greenhouse effect and increase advective heat transfer to the poles. A further surface warming results, which in turn causes more release of CO_2, augmenting the process further and continuing to increase the surface temperature to produce more CO_2. Eventually, it is hoped, atmospheric growth will become self-driving, the original engineered warming having been the trigger for a climatic runaway that terminates in a new, high-pressure, high-temperature regime. This is what these models have in common. Where they differ is in their assumptions as to the nature of the CO_2 reservoir and the engineering method chosen to destabilise it.

The first Martian terraforming models to be published in the technical literature were by Joseph Burns and Martin Harwit, and Carl Sagan, in 1973.[10] They were based on the now-obsolete 'long winter model' of the Martian climate postulating that up to 1 bar equivalent of CO_2 ice was stored in the polar caps, the episodic release of which was driven by the insolation changes brought about by the 50,000 year precession cycle of the planet's equinoxes.[11] Sagan speculated that the caps might be evaporated in just 100 years by artificially reducing their albedo, causing them to absorb more sunlight. A subsequent NASA study suggested that even a subtle darkening, a reduction in polar-cap albedo by just a few percent, from 0.77 to 0.73, might trigger runaway conditions.[12] Blanketing the polar ices with layers of dust, or by the growth of cold-adapted plants, were suggested as ways of effecting this darkening.[13] However, although the mass of dust indicated by Sagan's calculations did not appear prohibitive, the stability of any thin dust layer when subjected to attrition by the Martian winds is doubtful. As for the plants, none capable of survival and growth anywhere on the planet's surface are known.

Today, it seems that the Martian polar caps are composed principally of water ice with perhaps just a frosting of CO_2 or a mix in the form of CO_2 hydrate. There are doubts therefore that the caps have a rich enough store of CO_2 to satisfy the requirements of the model. However, it is possible that a far greater amount of CO_2 might lie adsorbed on mineral grains in the upper layers of the Martian regolith. Christopher McKay suggested that a modest heating of this source might serve to trigger a runaway release of CO_2 in an analogous manner to Sagan's model.[14] This early speculation has been explored further by computer

Notes
1 National Commission on Space, *Pioneering the Space Frontier*, Bantam Books (New York), 1986.
2 GK O'Neill, The High Frontier, Jonathan Cape Ltd (London) 1977; RD Johnson and C Holbrow, 'Space Settlements: A Design Study', NASA SP-413, 1977.
3 MJ Fogg, "Dynamics of a Terraformed Martian Biosphere', Journal of the British Interplanetary Society, 46, 1993, p283; Fogg, *Terraforming: Engineering Planetary Environments*, SAE International (Warrendale, PA), 1995.
4 J Williamson, writing as W Stewart, *Astounding Science Fiction*, XXIX(5), Collision Orbit (City?), 1942, p80.
5 L Brown, *The New Shorter Oxford English Dictionary*, vol 2, (N-Z), Clarendon Press (Oxford), 1993.
6 Fogg, *Terraforming: Engineering*, op cit.
7 Ibid.
8 Fogg, 'Terraforming Mars: Conceptual Solutions to the Problem of Plant Growth in Low Concentrations of Oxygen', J Brit Interplanet Soc, 48, 1995, p 427.
9 JB Pollack, JF Kasting, SM Richardson and K Poliakoff, 'The Case for a Wet, Warm Climate on Early Mars', *Icarus*, 94, 1, 1991.
10 JA Burns and M Harwit, 'Towards a More Habitable Mars – Or – The Coming Martian Spring', Icarus, 19, 1973, p 126; C Sagan, 'Planetary Engineering on Mars', Icarus, 20, 1973, p513.
11 Sagan, OB Toon and PJ Gierasch, 'Climatic Change on Mars', *Science*, 181, 1973, p1045.
12 MM Averner and RD MacElroy, 'On the Habitability of Mars: An Approach to Planetary Ecosynthesis', NASA SP-414, 1976.
13 Sagan, 'Planetary Engineering', op cit.
14 CP McKay, 'Terraforming Mars', Journal of the British Interplanetary Society, 35, 1982, p 427.

modelling.[15] It was shown that if the regolith carbon dioxide is distributed evenly over Mars, then the gas must be very loosely bound for any runaway to occur. For a polar regolith containing an equivalent of 1-bar CO_2 the effect works better: an initial warming of the Martian surface by 5–20 kelvin (depending on model parameters) increases the atmospheric pressure to a few tens of millibars. At this point, a runaway becomes established resulting in a stable end state of ~ 800 millibars and ~ 250 kelvin. A 2-bar reservoir would runaway to give a mean surface temperature of ~ 273 kelvin and a 3-bar reservoir, 280 kelvin.

James Lovelock and Michael Allaby suggested that regolith degassing could be triggered by releasing CFC gases into the Martian atmosphere to create an artificial greenhouse effect.[16] Since these chemicals have, molecule for molecule, a greenhouse effect 10,000 times that of CO_2, residence times of decades to centuries and are nontoxic, the idea at first sight appeared promising. McKay et al looked at this question in more detail, modelling a cocktail of CFC gases active in the infrared window region between 8–12 millimetre where CO_2 and water vapour have little absorption.[17] They found that a concentration of ~ 10 parts per million of such an absorber would be capable of warming Mars by about +30 kelvin, but that any temperature excursion in excess of this would be prevented by the increasing loss of heat from other spectral regions. However, they also noted that CFCs on Mars are far less stable and long-lived than on Earth, since UV radiation between 200–300 nanometres, which breaks the C-Cl bond, is not shielded from the surface by an ozone layer. Residence times for typical CFC molecules are reduced from many years to just hours. Thus, a CFC greenhouse on Mars might work (manufacturing the absolute quantity of trace gases appears feasible), if it were not for the fact that these gases would require replenishment at an absurd rate. A solution to this problem might be to use perfluoro compounds instead, as the C-F bond is much more robust. Perfluorocarbons are so inert they can survive conditions on Mars, but most of their relevant absorption bands, at least for compounds of three carbon atoms or more, appear to be unpublished. Whether it will be possible to use perfluorocarbons to greenhouse Mars remains an open question.[18]

Another way to warm Mars would be to increase its input of solar energy by reflecting light that passes the planet down to its surface.

The use of orbiting mirrors to do this is a frequent suggestion in terraforming-related discussions[19] and some outline designs have been published.[20] Whilst all are necessarily large in size, none are unfeasible in principle and their masses are surprisingly modest. A mirror system specifically designed as part of a runaway-greenhouse scenario was presented by Robert Zubrin and McKay. By balancing gravitational and light-pressure forces, they determined that a 125-kilometre-diameter solar sail-mirror could be stationed 214,000 kilometres behind Mars, where it could illuminate the south pole with an additional ~ 27 terawatts. This

15 McKay, OB Toon and JF Kasting, 'Making Mars Habitable', Nature, 352, 1991, p489; R Zubrin and McKay, 'Technological Requirements for Terraforming Mars', AIAA-93-2005, 1993.
16 JE Lovelock and M Allaby, The Greening of Mars, Warner Brothers Inc (New York), 1984.
17 McKay, 'Does Mars Have Rights? An Approach to the Environmental Ethics of Planetary Engineering', in D MacNiven (ed) Moral Expertise, Routledge (London and New York), 1990, pp184–97.
18 Fogg, Terraforming: Engineering, op cit.
19 For example JE Oberg, New Earths, New American Library Inc (New York), 1981.
20 P Birch, 'Terraforming Mars Quickly', Journal of the British Interplanetary Society, 45, 1992, p331; Zubrin and McKay, 'Technological Requirements', op cit; Fogg, Terraforming: Engineering, op cit.

21 Averner and MacElroy, 'On the Habitability', op cit; McKay et al, 'Making Mars Habitable', op cit.
22 Fogg, 'Dynamics', op cit; Fogg, *Terraforming: Engineering*, op cit.
23 Fogg 'The Creation of an Artificial Dense Martian Atmosphere: A Major Obstacle to the Terraforming of Mars', J Brit Interplanet Soc, 42, 1989, p 577; Fogg, 'A Synergic Approach to Terraforming Mars, J Brit Interplanet Soc, 45, 1992, p 315.
24 Birch, 'Terraforming Mars Quickly', op cit.
25 Zubrin and McKay, 'Technological Requirements', op cit.
26 Fogg, 'A Synergic Approach', op cit; Fogg, *Terraforming: Engineering*, op cit.
27 VR Baker, RG Strom, VC Gulick, JS Kargel, G Komatsu and VS Kale, 'Ancient Oceans, Ice Sheets and the Hydrological Cycle on Mars', *Nature*, 352, 1991, p 589.
28 Fogg, 'A Synergic Approach', op cit; Fogg, *Terraforming: Engineering*, op cit.
29 SM Clifford, 'A Model for the Hydrologic and Climatic Behaviour of Water on Mars', *J Geophys Res*, 98, 1993, p 10973.
30 Fogg, 'The Ethical Dimensions of Space Settlement', IAA-99-IAA.7.1.07, presented at the 50th International Astronautical Congress, Amsterdam, 1999.
31 Fogg 'Terraforming: A Review for Environmentalists, *The Environmentalist*, 13, 1993, p 7; Fogg, *Terraforming: Engineering*, op cit.
32 El Friedmann, M Hua and R Ocampo-Friedmann, 'Terraforming Mars: Dissolution of Carbonate Rocks by Cyanobacteria', Journal of the British Interplanetary Society, 46, 1993, p 291.
33 Averner and MacElroy, 'On the Habitability', op cit; JA Hiscox and DJ Thomas, 'Genetic Modification and Selection of Micro-organisms for Growth on Mars, Journal of the British Interplanetary Society, 48, 1995, p 419.

An earlier version of this paper was published in *Advances in Space Research*, 22 (3), 1998, pp 415–420 and is reprinted with permission.

Opposite
Esther De Angelis,
Exotic Science

should be sufficient to raise the polar temperature by ~ 5 kelvin which, according to some models, should be sufficient for cap evaporation. At first glance, the size of such a mirror and its mass (200,000 tons of aluminium) may appear too grandiose a concept to take seriously. However, such a mass is equivalent to just five days worth of the Earth's production of aluminium, and whilst it would be impractical to ship this from the Earth, there seems no reason why it might not be obtained by mining and manufacturing in space. The first space mirror has already been tested in Earth orbit (the Russian 20 metre Znamia project) and vastly larger variants are possible about Mars. If sufficient CO_2 is produced by their heating of the planet's poles, then this might act as the trigger for a much more extensive regolith degassing.

Problems and Alternatives

Runaway-greenhouse scenarios of terraforming promise much: that through comparatively modest engineering (at a level far less than the integrated activity of humanity on the Earth) Mars can be transformed into a planet habitable for anaerobic life in roughly a century. Conditions would still be hostile, akin to an arid and chilly Precambrian, but far less so than at present. Further terraforming might follow ecopoiesis by, for example, arranging for photosynthesis to oxygenate the atmosphere. Long time scales of 100,000 years have been cited for this step,[21] although it appears reasonable that this might be reduced by at least a factor of 10 if the biosphere is actively managed to optimise net oxygen production.[22]

Although the runaway greenhouse is considered the pre-eminent model, it has been subject to useful criticism and suggestions of engineering alternatives. It seems quite possible (perhaps likely) that if Mars' original inventory of CO_2 remains on the planet, then it will have ended up for the most part chemically bound in carbonate minerals, rather than physically bound as the more labile CO_2 ice or regolith adsorbate. If this is the case, then re-release of this paleoatmosphere will require extremely energetic processes such as devolatilisation of carbonate strata by buried nuclear explosives,[23] heat beams,[24] or asteroid impacts.[25] Such activities planetwide would be highly destructive and are difficult to countenance.

Another problem is to do with water – the surface of Mars must be moist to be habitable. Although Mars has visible reserves of water in the polar caps and may have an abundance in the shallow subsurface north and south of 30 degrees latitude, it is difficult to make this available to any biosphere. The slow pace of heat conduction through regolith would greatly delay the melting of permafrost and it could be millennia before an appreciable quantity of water has pooled at low elevations.[26] There are potential ways around this problem, given that flash floods have occurred naturally on Mars, perhaps great enough to have rapidly flooded the northern plains.[27] Should source aquifers still exist, then it may be possible to destabilise them and duplicate this outburst flooding, but again, the engineering required might be violent and unacceptable to many.[28] However, a recent detailed model of the Martian hydrological cycle suggests that the lowest regions on Mars might be underlain by aquifers under artesian pressure.[29] If this is the case, then there is hope for the rapid creation of lowland lakes with little more hardware than pumps and drilling rigs.[30]

Conclusions

At present, all research into planetary engineering, whether applied to Mars or anywhere else, is concerned entirely with defining the boundaries of the possible, rather than in charting some definite route into the future. The concept can no longer be described as fantasy, although confirmation of its practicality awaits a detailed exploration of Mars. Further exploration will clarify an inventory of its resources, a better understanding of the phenomenon of planetary habitability and a future where the solar system is opened to technological civilisation as a new and expanding frontier.

Apart from its possible role as a long-range goal for space exploration, today such work is valuable as a stimulating, interdisciplinary thought experiment with uses in education, terrestrial planetology and the entertainment media.[31] The range of subjects potentially within its remit is large. Recent interest has been shown in identifying species of cold and desiccation-resistant microorganisms that might be assembled into the first ecosystems to pioneer the Red Planet.[32] The potential of genetically engineering even hardier 'Marsbugs' is being discussed.[33] If terraforming is possible, then ought it to be permitted? Can changing the face of a planet represent a moral act? What if extant life is found within still warm, deep-seated, Martian aquifers? The extension of earthbound environmental ethics into a cosmic setting opens up whole new areas of philosophical and cultural debate.

Currently, though, we cannot say whether life can really take hold on the Red Planet. We know too little about Mars, and not enough about the Earth and its habitability. To find out for certain, we will probably have to send humans to explore the planet as part of living there. ⌂

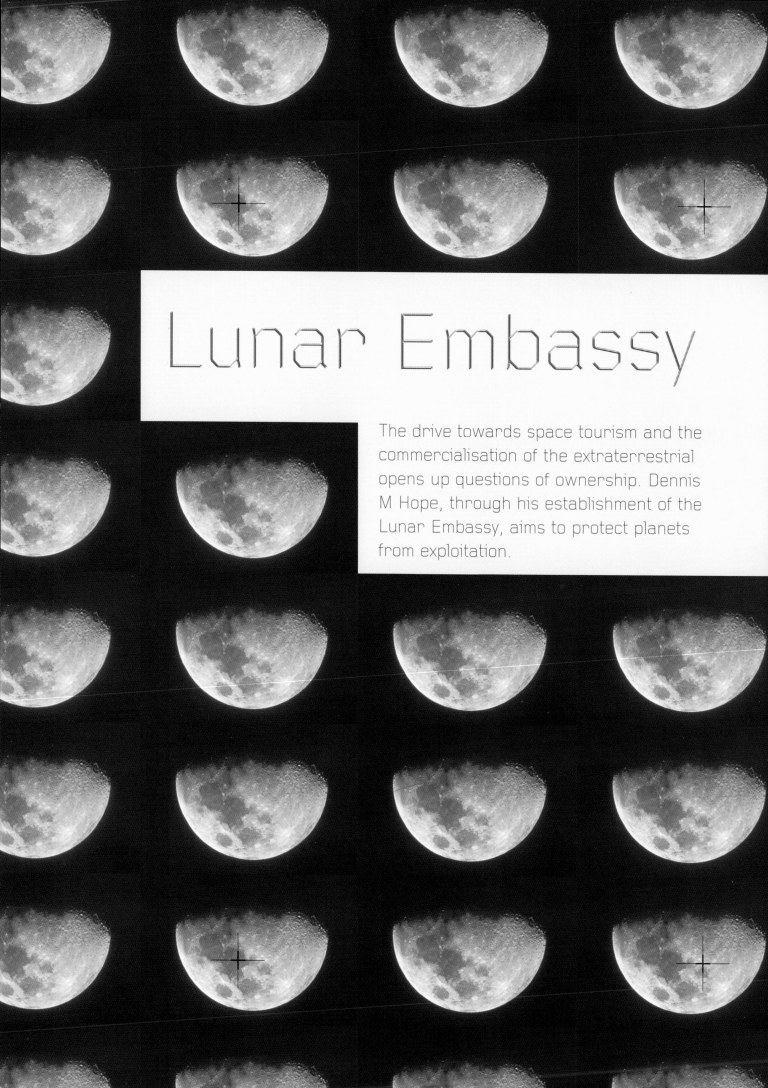

Lunar Embassy

The drive towards space tourism and the commercialisation of the extraterrestrial opens up questions of ownership. Dennis M Hope, through his establishment of the Lunar Embassy, aims to protect planets from exploitation.

Lunar Embassy, the founders and leaders in extraterrestrial real estate, is the only company in the world recognised as possessing a legal basis and copyright for selling and registering extra-terrestrial estates on the Moon, Mars, Venus and Io.

Contrary to popular opinion and a great deal of general misinformation on this subject, it is possible to own a piece of another planet or moon in our solar system. The sale of lunar property has been ongoing since 1980 through the Lunar Embassy, following a declaration of ownership by Mr Dennis M Hope for the Moon of Earth and the other eight planets and their moons. This claim was filed with the United Nations, the USA and the former Soviet Union. There are now over 100,000 lunar property-owners from all walks of life. It is definitely a growing market, with an average of 129 properties being sold daily. Once you have bought your piece of lunar real estate the Lunar Embassy will give you the exact coordinates of your property so that when you get to the Moon, you can just go to the longitude and latitude of your land and set up camp.

Two treaties currently in existence concern the sale of extraterrestrial property: the Outer Space Treaty of 1967 and the Moon Treaty of 1984. These treaties do not refer to 'ownership' as such; they more commonly refer to the 'exploitation of the Moon and other celestial bodies for profit purposes'. Extraterrestrial property sales distinctly fall under this definition.

The Outer Space Treaty of 1967 explicitly forbids any government from claiming a celestial resource such as the Moon or a planet. By signing this treaty, governments have effectively waived their rights to these bodies. However, most importantly, the Outer Space Treaty does not exempt commercial enterprises or private individuals from making claim to, exploiting or appropriating these celestial bodies for profit.

Very soon after the UN and other nations signed the Outer Space Treaty they became aware of this vital omission, and tried to ratify an amendment to include corporations and individuals. Unfortunately, all attempts at ratifying such an amendment failed because many member states did not agree with it, resulting in the famous Moon Treaty which was drawn up some 15 years later.

This forbids the exploitation of space, the Moon and other celestial bodies for profit motives. According to the treaty, individuals may not claim the Moon and other celestial bodies. However, out of approximately 185 member states of the UN, only six states supported the Moon Treaty. All the others, including all spacefaring nations such as the USA, Russia and China, refused to sign it and did not sign it. The USA at the time said that it would prefer to wait and see 'how public opinion develops'. Worryingly, some influential sources, including NASA's own published archives actually incorrectly list the Moon Treaty as ratified.

The Lunar Embassy believes that prohibiting private individuals and corporations from making claims to extraterrestrial property is not in the public interest and by selling real estate in these locations, it is not breaking any existing laws.

Many companies are gearing up to exploit lunar and celestial resources for profit. NASA, the Robotics Institute and LunaCorp plans to launch the first 'private' mission to the Moon, the Lunar Rover Initiative, in 1999. The intention is to put several remote-controlled buggies on to the Moon and participants on Earth will be able to make contact with a lunar robot using virtual reality helmets and cruise across the lunar surface. These companies could not develop such a theme park if it was illegal by any treaty to exploit the Moon for profit motives. Moreover, private investors would not put over $900 million into such a project if the companies were affiliated with governments, as NASA is, because the Outer Space Treaty would prohibit their actions.

Currently no law exists on any other planet or moon in our solar system except here on Earth. If private individuals and corporations settle on the Moon and Mars, for example, laws must be established to ensure people's rights. This cannot be accomplished unless ownership rights are addressed and settled.

Some lobbyists suggest that ownership should be linked to the proximity of the individual to the property in question. That means if you have the money to go there, you can have it. The Lunar Embassy thinks this is not a good idea, because it would give precedence to corporations and financially capable organisations to file and receive an extraterrestrial property. Ordinary people would therefore forfeit any claims if such a suggestion were followed: it is much more difficult, physically and financially, for us to reach the Moon or the other eight planets.

The Lunar Embassy aims to help to protect the right of the public should space law be established, and allow everyone to claim and use extraterrestrial resources, regardless of their proximity to the property.

The Moon and celestial bodies are for all of us to enjoy. They symbolise hope, romance, achievement and change, all rolled into one. In addition, they even light up at night! There is nothing more symbolic and romantic on Earth than to give a loved one part of the heavens. It is not a fad we can toy with; it is not something that will ever lose its appeal. When you buy your property on the Moon or any other planet please enjoy it – that is what this is really all about. ◮

Sci-Fi Modernism

Space-Age Retro

A whole generation of architects, whose childhood imaginations were fuelled by sci fi visions of the Space Age on TV and in film, are now realising their fantasies through their design. Edwin Heathcote explains how these architects have been looking back in order to look forwards.

Nothing dates faster than the future, yet it is the nostalgic visions of the future which are fuelling some of the most interesting modern designs. It is a new kind of retro-futuristic historicism. Just as the fashions of our youth are exhumed to feed the imaginations of revival-hungry designers, the space-age fantasies that pervaded architects' childhoods are returning to haunt our modern cities.

My childhood was saturated with futuristic images of underwater and supersonic marionettes (*Thunderbirds*, *Stingray*, et al), saving the world from the goings-on in secret, hangar-like bases carved from the rocks; James Bond baddies trying to hold the world to ransom from hangar-like bases carved into volcanoes; and Batman emerging from a futuristic hangar-like cave in his Batmobile to save the world from being held to ransom by baddies in hangar-like bases. The war-room in *Dr Strangelove* (Kubrick, 1963), the Death Star in *Star Wars* (Lucas, 1977), the Batcave, Dr No's hide-out, *Thunderbirds'* Tracey Island, Ming the Merciless's control room – evil was personified by enormous spaces (preferably subterranean to give that metaphorical hint of hell), lit by banks of flashing lights.

The 1960s and the TV series and films that fuelled my childhood were dominated by a vision of space that was somewhere between *Barbarella* (1967) and *The Jetsons*. It was a curious blend of psychedelia and cartoon humour. The more serious films that dealt with space were actually more concerned with inner space and the mind, from Tarkovsky's *Solaris* (1972) to Kubrick's *2001* (1968), where the settings were the background to paranoia and existential angst, or the cause of it in the case of HAL, Kubrick's omnipresent computer.

The notions of space and technology that defined our childhood fantasies have survived remarkably well. The Van der Graaf generators that dominated the laboratory of every self-respecting mad scientist and the lava lamps that once adorned the baddies' lairs can now be found in every gift shop, staples of the kitsch market. Our archive of childhood filmic images, those cheesy sets and dubious spaceships, provide a mine of references. There were the Art Deco space rockets in 1930s *Flash Gordon* Saturday morning specials, spewing sparks and smoke as they rose into the sky (on strings), and Ming the Merciless's base, replete with armies of slaves shovelling coal into great furnaces.

By contrast, the 1970s revival of *Buck Rogers in the 21st Century* looked as if it was set in some kind of souped-up Studio 54. *Star Wars* functioned in the same kind of sterilised vision of space, though to someone of Corbusier's generation, the Death Star was the ultimate dream: a whole planet to design. The parallel with Hitler's Berlin was obvious. It was almost the last gasp of sci-fi Modernism before the genre degenerated into the organic, dangerous darkness of Ridley Scott's *Alien* (1979), designed by HR Giger, and its sequels: truly disturbing visions of life 'out there'. We can trace the exposed ducts and wiring of All Bar One or Pret a Manger, the industrial chic of lofts and the corporate and public acceptance of High-tech back to this tubular, ad hoc vision of the space station as a less than perfect space in which to live, dominated by services rather than aesthetics.

Then came Postmodernism. In the early 1980s, retro set design based on forms drawn from the past, less dominated by technology and expressing a more cynical, bleaker view of the world, became the new futuristic cool. The trend, it could be argued, began with *Planet of the Apes* (1967), which depicted the future as a tragic, postapocalyptic landscape. In the 1980s, it gathered pace, inspired by dark, Kafkaesque visions of a stark, bureaucratic future. The sets for Terry Gilliam's *Brazil* (1985) and Tim Burton's *Batman* (1989) looked to Art Deco and nightmarish, urban imagery. The future no longer resembled the Hawaiian island paradise of *Thunderbirds* or *The Lost Planet*; it was more like the back alleys of a North American dystopia, starved of light by gargantuan buildings within which hatted and overcoated extras from *noir* films scurried around with their collars turned up to the cold. To these could be added the vision of London as a war-ravaged battleground, as seen in George Orwell's *1984*,

all 1940s typewriters and cheap cigarettes. Gilliam's hilarious ducted interior landscapes (spewing forth their guts like offal) and hopelessly unreliable machines, gave us a future (like Winston Smith's in *1984*) of bureaucracy and drudgery, of battling against machines that hindered rather than helped us. It was a dysfunctional future to which we could relate.

In the 1990s, as outerspace became more accessible and we began to know more about the origins of the cosmos, we found that we do not want what seems to be the reality: dusty planets and the dense nothingness of black holes. We preferred the nostalgic optimism of B-movie Martians and the exciting possibilities of faults in the system, like wormholes and meteors (see *Event-Horizon* 1997, *Armageddon* 1998, etc). Invaders from space were no longer the 1950s body-snatcher models, metaphors for Communists in a paranoid Cold War. They were light-hearted figures of fun, like cuddly, doe-eyed *ET* (1982), the wonderful, destructive-but-cute, laugh-as-you-blast space-aliens of Tim Burton's *Mars Attacks* (1996) or the comic SFX creatures of *Men in Black* (1997). When Po-mo begat irony, the space age became a repository of knowing, futuristic images, blended with a little punk and a splash of 1950s Sputnik modern. The same appeal fills auction houses with collectable tin robots and ray guns, and has made silver a fashionable colour.

In architecture, the notion of futuristic cities that had been explored in the films of the 1920s and 1930s, notably Fritz Lang's vision of the *Metropolis* (1926) and Moholy Nagy's total environment in *Things to Come* (1936), was being explored in the 1960s, partly prompted by environmental fears and anxiety about nuclear war. With the stars and stripes firmly planted on the surface of the moon, the idea of creating a brave new world on another planet began to appear a realistic alternative in the light of impending catastrophe. Archigram and the Metabolists were creating whole environments that looked as though they had not only come from another planet, but should be erected there. These self-supporting, total structures, their guts and organs on the outside, led inexorably towards the Centre Pompidou, the Lloyds Building (both oozing space-station chic) and the High-tech superbuildings. The musings of Peter Cook and Ron Herron may have been humorous, but they were not entirely inconceivable. They were as much a part of the swinging London scene as inflatable furniture and plastic bubble chairs. Ironically, though, it is the latter that have survived to become design icons, and inflatable architecture remains all the rage. It was recently the subject of a show at RIBA, and Nigel Coates's showcase for Cool Britannia, *power:house*, consisted of a blow-up expo. Even James Bond's new gadget in *The World Is Not Enough* (1999), is an inflatable coat that blows up into a protective capsule.

In fact, Coates has been highly instrumental in the development of modern sci-fi space chic. His stainless-steel flying saucers at the Sheffield Centre for Popular Music (1998) have created a spacey aesthetic in the northern postindustrial landscape – part of a wider, emerging aesthetic that blends retro sci fi with high-tech materials and forms. This seems to have been developed over the last few years with the 1950s rocket-shape of Philippe Starck's lemon-juicer, for example, or the resurrection of modular furniture and laboratory-white interiors studded with Op Art. The new look can be seen in the work of both young designers and old masters. Oscar Niemayer's Niterói Art Gallery (Brazil, 1991–96), with its flying-saucer gallery and Star Trek

Coates has created a spacey aesthetic in the northern post-industrial landscape – part of a wider, emerging aesthetic that blends retro sci fi with high-tech materials and forms

wraparound window, is among the finest and most profound of these designs, while at the commercial level, Misha Stefan's futuristic Fluid juice bars, all PVC and 1970s rounded corners, take these ideas to the public. In a move away from Coates's early ducts and wiring interiors, where everything was exposed (a notion that can be seen in its extreme form in both the *Alien* films and the fantasies of Lebbeus Woods), the current crop of spacey structures is returning to the streamlined era of fictional space travel, when surfaces were smooth and interiors white. Ushida Findlay have long been investigating this kind of design: their Soft and Hairy House (Tokyo, 1994) and Truss Wall House (Tokyo, 1992) set the trend for swirling, blobby sci-fi forms (they remind me of Woody Allen's Orgasmatron in *Sleeper,* 1973). Jan Kaplicky and Future Systems have been expounding their version of this futuristic vision for even longer – the recent Lords Media Centre (1999) is perhaps the

Opposite and above
Branson Coates, Sheffield
Centre for Popular Music, 1998.
Nigel Coates's stainless-steel
flying saucers have created
a fittingly at once retro and
futuristic image for a pop centre.

best example of sci-fi chic to be seen anywhere. Blending real structural innovation with the white UFO aesthetic, Kaplicky really is creating new forms and structures with the simplicity and rigidity of the monocoque form used by boatbuilders. His recent domestic houses are also excellent examples of this new spacey version of High-tech, organic futurism. Even Richard Rogers' Greenwich Dome, the trademark of the Millennium, seems to take its aesthetic from the UFO (as does the Teletubbies' ecofriendly turf-covered home), and the future of the domestic house at the 1998 *Daily Mail Ideal Home Exhibition* (both newspaper and exhibition staunch bastions of suburban gnome-and-net-curtain culture) was seen as Nigel Coates's super-sci-fi Oyster House.

As we passed 1999 (remember the Moon bases in 'Space 1999'?) and embarked on 2000 (remember 'Judge Dredd' and '2000 AD'?) anticipating 2001, where we probably won't encounter much of a space odyssey, real spacecraft look about as dynamic and convincing as the space hoppers on which we bounced around. When we see pictures of the now-defunct Mir, we see not the hygienic white hospital interiors of the space station in Kubrick's fantasy, but sardine-can space-tips, all stuck together with duct tape and coated in tin foil like yesterday's sandwich wrappings. It is a vision closer to *The Clangers* than to *Barbarella*. The design of spacecraft has changed little since the space shuttle appeared as a cutting-edge prop in James Bond's 1979 outing, *Moonraker*. The shuttle itself appears clumsy and (particularly after the Challenger disaster) not the sort of thing in which we're likely to reach the stars. Satellites and space stations are inelegant chunks of metal with big, flappy solar panels, which sometimes fail to open. It is not as glamorous as we might have wished.

Perhaps the answer is to create an alternative using images of how the space age should have looked. Despite having passed 1999 and approaching 2001, we still have no Moonbases, we have met no Martians and we do not commute to work dressed in silver suits and driving hovercars. In fact, internal combustion engines and lounge suits still look pretty much the same as they did 70 years ago. What the space age and science fiction have given us is an image, and it is that image, a fantasy of the future rather than the reality of the year 2000, that is propelling design forward. What the space age and science fiction has left us is an image, and it is that image, a fantasy of the future rather than the reality of the year 2000, that is propelling design forward. Simultaneously cutting-edge and Kitsch, sci-fi architecture is a curious blend of nostalgia, disappointment and optimism that architecture can still present a vision of the future which can entertain, delight and stir up fond memories of what the world could have been like. ⌂

UR-BOOR

A Rachel Rosenthal Performance

A work in progress by the performance artist Rachel Rosenthal provokes us to consider whether we should be setting the Earth in order before we try to go to space in technological contraptions.

Rachel Rosenthal's work investigates the interconnectedness of all things, be they human, transhuman, planetary or cosmic. The performance piece, Ur-Boor, is a work in progress. A new, final solo, commissioned by the government of Quebec, which will be performed with an interactive, musical set, will tour in the year 2000. The set is by Guy Laramee, who has designed for *Angels in America* and Robert LePage; Amy Knoles, a member of the California EAR Unit, and an international musician, has devised the sound and music.

The piece is set on a space station in the future and explores the relationship between politeness and violence, from manners at European courts to the current boorishness in the media and entertainment industries, via interaction with a musical, catapulting environment of insult, obstacle and challenge. Rosenthal portrays a human scapegoat, sent into space in a strange, organic capsule to embody and exorcise the Ur-Boor, the global personification of our incivility, grossness and lack of manners. Halfway through the performance, she sneezes and a chip comes out of her nose revealing that her space adventures are just an illusion and that she is really in a dirty backyard that could be in downtown LA. As she starts to clear up the debris things begin to grow, and the capsule becomes a sort of gazebo, covered in immense flowers, courtesy of New York painter LC Armstrong.

The ending is very ambiguous, leaving us with a reality that may or may not be virtual. The courtyard may be virtual, not the space capsules. We don't know for sure. ⌀

Photo: Annie Leibovitz

Photo Credit: Annie Leibovitz

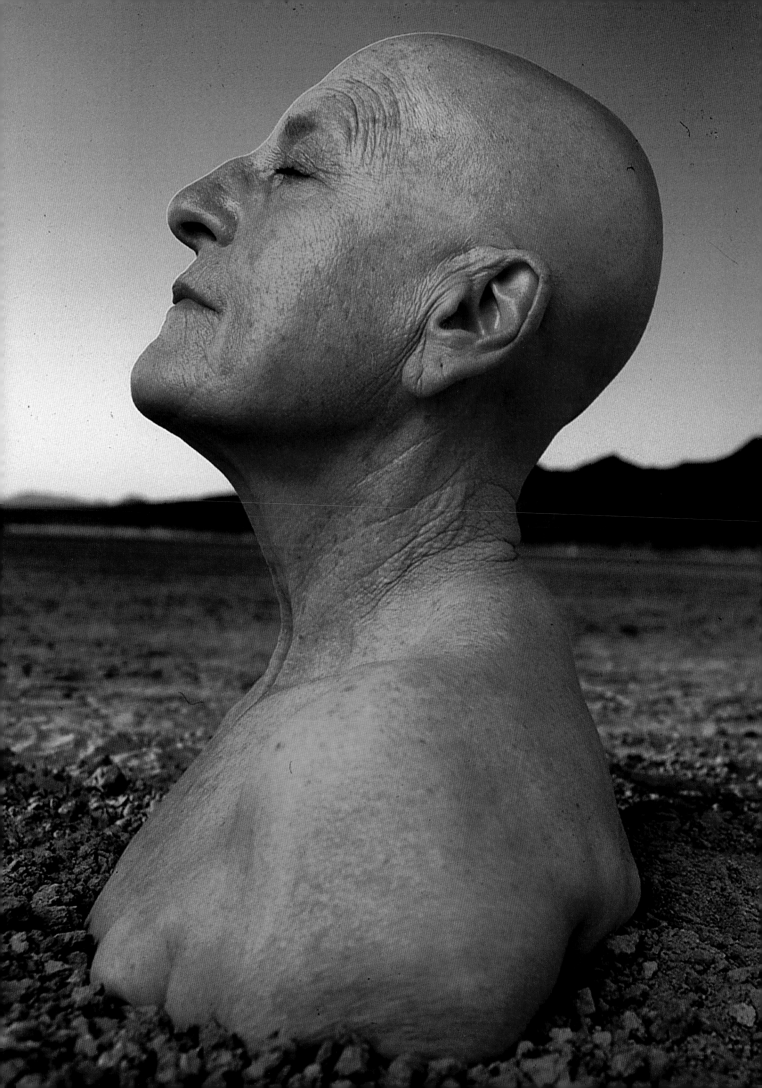

Space Architecture

The Bartlett School of Architecture, University College London, has achieved international recognition, both for its teaching and for its research. Here, we summarise a discussion between a group of experts from the Bartlett, who speculate on the implications of space habitation.

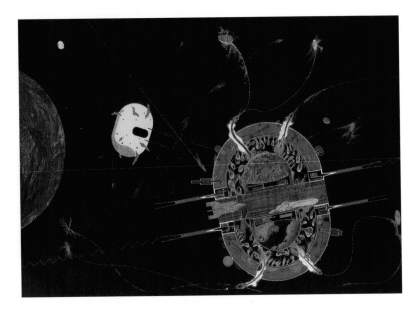

Above and over page
Peter Cook, design for
a space resort, 2000.

At the Bartlett School of Architecture, renowned for 'thinking the unthinkable', a group of radicals including Dr Rachel Armstrong, Professor Peter Cook, Professor Colin Fournier, Stephen Gage, Neil Spiller and Charles Walker, met to address the challenges faced by our civilisation over the next 50 years. The Bartlett brainstorming reflected on all aspects of the future of the built environment, from where we will live to the incorporation of artificial intelligence and new materials. Naturally, one of the subjects addressed was the question of space habitation. For these academics and practitioners of architecture, the challenges of an extraterrestrial location were not beyond their architectural remits, since none of the technical architectural solutions that will be used to create the first public spaces in orbit will be new. 'We need not await successful revolutions in technology to solve the problems of today's high costs of access to space, nor do we need to deprive ourselves of their benefits should they occur.' [Starcraft Boosters, Inc, The StarBooster 200 System, a Cargo Aircraft for Space, prepared for AIAA/ASME/SAE Joint Propulsion Specialists' Conference, 22 June 1999, Los Angeles, CA, by Dr Buzz Aldrin and Hubert P Davis.]

Space as Utopia

Few places on Earth exist that have not been subject to the aspirations of architects, but perhaps the greatest conceptual challenge is the space beyond our own planet. Since the beginning of human civilisation, we have given the heavens structure in the form of celestial maps and astrological charts. Religious icons and the hieroglyphics of ancient Egypt have reflected the inspiration we derive from the skies. But until the 20th century, they were way beyond our reach.

The inaccessibility of locations has never stopped pioneers from speculating on how they may look and be reached and used by human beings. Artists and writers have often invented such speculative, entirely new worlds. Most famous, is the treatise *Utopia* by Thomas More, who coined this term, deriving from Greek and meaning 'no place', as the name of his idealised community. Utopias are imaginary places, societies or worlds that do not exist but could plausibly be created given access and unlimited resources. Those designed by architects tend to reflect the latest technological inventions and philosophies of the era.

Life in space promises a utopian ideal that weaves together many topical cultural aspirations in science, technology and human relationships. We fantasise that in the extraterrestrial environment we will be freed from the histories and legacies of the old world, and will be able to reinvent ourselves. We look to distant locations for solutions, to escape from problems such as overcrowding, pollution, war and the destruction of the Earth.

In *The High Frontier: Human Colonies in Space*, Gerard K O'Neill sought to explain how by the 1990s human colonies would be manning satellites halfway between the Earth and the Moon, pioneering the construction of solar power stations to supply inexhaustible energy to the Earth.[1] O'Neill also outlines how life styles will be shaped by these artificial environments, how climate, gravity, day-length and conditions for family life will evolve, speculating that in 200 years there could be more people living in space than on Earth.

Global Politics and Economics
The main obstacle to realising Professor O'Neill's vision has been the failure of governments to invest in space programmes that serve anything other than a military purpose. Space is a political issue before it is an economic concern. It not only reflects cultural agendas, but also unifies nations, symbolising the redemption of the human race in the event of a global catastrophe.

Since the Moon landings, the iconography of the planet Earth as seen from orbit has become a powerful symbol of international harmony and peaceful collaboration between nations. This beacon of human achievement has taken on a religious dimension and will become increasingly important as a symbol of unity as the global economy goes through its first set of major problems in the third millennium.

The principal difficulties appear to be the impending collapse of the Eastern economy and the prospect of nuclear war in Asia as Islamic countries resist the domination of the planet by a new world order orchestrated by Western superpowers.

With the end of the Cold War, the military forces of Western civilisation require a new role, and at the turn of the millennium a phenomenological milestone needs to be reached. Globalisation reflects a political shift towards international politics, by definition a shift that allows people to feel part of a larger whole, with world trade and the reversal of pollution and the depletion of the Earth's resources as the unifying goal. With the advent of technological progress and increasingly successful space missions, the public has been made aware that the planet as a whole, and not just ecology and infrastructure, is at peril.

There are two main scenarios for the future of the human race, both involving a great deal of risk. First, we can remain on this planet and eventually poison ourselves, blow ourselves to bits competing for territory or possibly experience destruction by a meteor. Second, we can leave the planet and speciate the universe. The question that our civilisation should be asking is not when space travel for civilians will happen, but why it has not happened earlier? After all, the Apollo 11 Moon landing took place a generation ago.

The first objection to space exploration is capital investment. With the advent of reusable craft, however, the cost of a space launch will decrease. The threshold for private investment will be reached when the world's multinationals, who already spend billions of dollars on advertising, consider the sponsorship of orbital craft and stations better value for money: space events currently guarantee extensive international media coverage. Advertising stunts and logos such as that commissioned for Beagle 2's launch to Mars would be likely investments. Beagle 2 is exploiting the reinvention of Britain's image under Tony Blair's New Labour as Cool Britannia by selecting the artist Damien Hirst, leader of the 'Brit pack' of talented creatives, to design a 'universally recognisable' logo, like a transmission test-card for the side of the craft. The combination of art world *enfant terrible* and the excitement that surrounds a voyage to the Red Planet has already produced many hours of high-profile media coverage.

Having a presence in orbit is the ultimate status symbol, providing a literal, metaphorical and virtual image of unlimited potential. The new millennium will increasingly reveal complex relationships between people and space, relating to a variety of physical, informational, metaphorical and virtual territories. Corporations will hope to be regarded as in some way embodying a utopian ideal, marketing not products but life styles, which will be branded and even insured, on behalf of a spectrum of investors. These may include

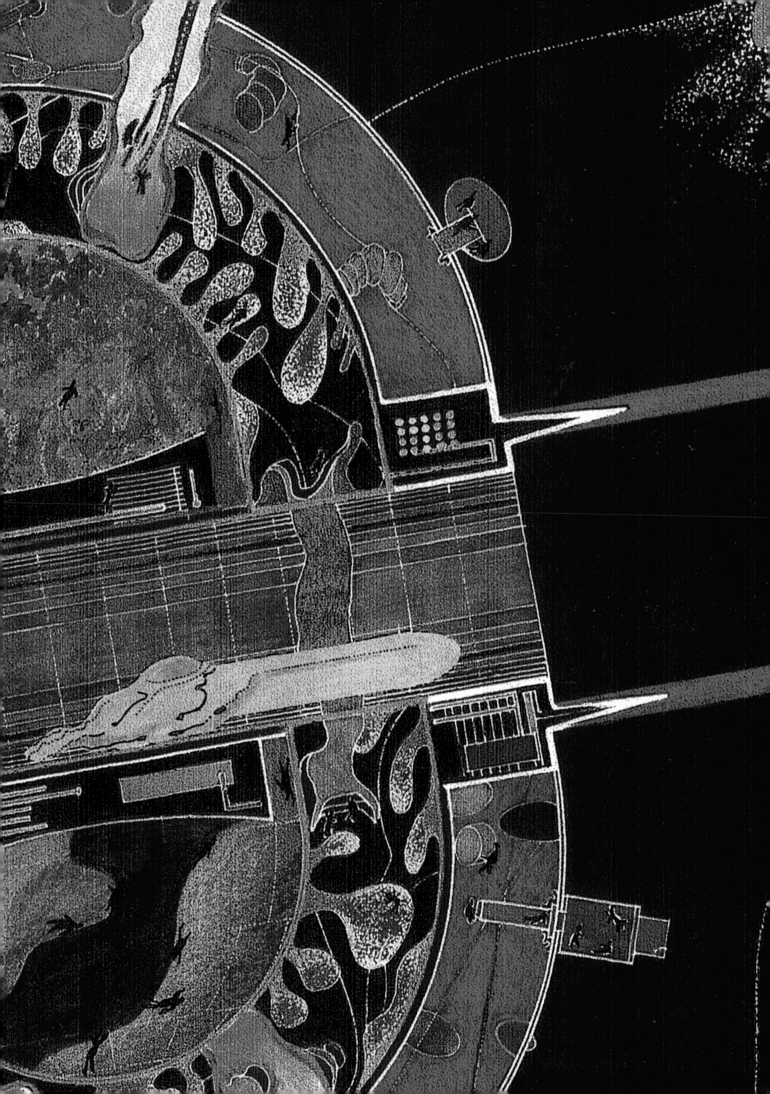

manufacturers, pharmaceutical companies and banks, who can agree on a united 'life style package' that will represent a particular philosophy and guarantee a certain quality of life for consumers. In the new century, we will see a proliferation of branded satellites, laser projections on to asteroids and insignia on spacecraft, brought back into our domestic worlds through the digital screen.

Communications Research

In space, the possibility of an encounter with an alien species will be ever present. Enthusiasts such as the NASA-endorsed organisation SETI (search for extraterrestrial intelligence) have been scanning the skies for contact with extraterrestrial beings for decades, pushing forward the boundaries for interplanetary communications systems and broadening our understanding of the signals coming to us from the universe.

New frequencies and means of communicating across huge distances will be established, and an interplanetary Internet system (Inter-Planet) is already under way. Information and communications in space will have their own highways, frequencies and architectures, rather like the flight pathways of aeroplanes. There will be intelligent robots and satellites to position the nodes of contact and to lay down the communications superhighways. It may be necessary to negotiate with these surveillance systems – which can be thought of as automated pilots or 'space dolphins' – if they are given artificial intelligence.

Ecology and Speciation

In the absence of natural microflora and fauna in spacecraft, the role of commensals and balanced ecosystems will be an essential design issue in space architecture since, as the human body is not a monoculture, it is not possible to create a completely sterile spacecraft. Human flesh is crawling with microbes and bacteria and in the absence of natural forces, such as abundant water for cleansing, wind for circulating fresh air, it may be possible for normally harmless organisms to produce illness and disease. It will therefore be important to ensure that natural commensal and symbiotic microorganisms are introduced into spacecraft and encouraged to thrive in orbit.

When we begin to stay for longer, it will be necessary to bring other species into orbit and establish mature ecosystems. It is likely that we will want to grow crops in orbit to reduce

the transport cost of food. These may be designer organisms that are a cross between animal, vegetable and intelligent surfaces. The intelligent surfaces could act as a source of water, minerals and artificial light. This would fuel the growth of algae and bacteria, which can be made into a variety of different products with minimum processing.

Building in Space

Space travel provides the ultimate challenge for designers and architects wishing to create an environment that is self-contained and can grow with, and is seamlessly integrated with, the human beings it protects and nurtures. One of the major challenges will be to identify substances that will be cheap and easy to assemble in space. Spacecraft and space stations will be assembled like Lego. The basic units will be manufactured from all over the world and will have standardised electrical circuitry, oxygen-carbon-dioxide-nitrogen-mixture carrying capacities, internal pressure, etc, in order to prevent negative external forces ripping environments apart.

The less human intervention and maintenance of space structures there is, the less costly habitation will be. Smart materials that are capable of self-repair will be needed, as the cost of sending up repair crews could prove prohibitive to future space stations. Not all materials will need to be artificial. Some organic materials that can grow, divide and mature in space, like bone, could be used to grow space stations from the culture of cellular 'seeds'.

To avoid disorientation, buildings able to maintain their own life cycles, mimicking the diurnal Earth patterns of sleeping and waking, and which can recycle water and organic products, will be necessary to pacify their inhabitants psychologically.

The ideal architectural material to use in a vacuum is, of course, light. Laser highways, sculptures, artworks and advertising will be part of the information and architectural structure of colonised space.

Art and Space

Artists will be sponsored and commissioned to make a new kind of public art – works geared to a leisure-seeking, extraterrestrial community on space holiday. These site-specific artworks will humanise the extraterrestrial desert and serve to test new communications, construction and image-making technologies.

The French choreographer, Kitsou Dubois, has already danced during a parabolic flight on the space shuttle, and artist Cornelia Parker has made public her desire to put a fallen meteorite back into the extraterrestrial atmosphere on one of the scheduled space flights. As televisual networks are extended into orbit, live coverage of events will guarantee exposure for commissioners of extraterrestrial artwork and remote viewers will enable terrestrial viewers to browse the antigravity gallery.

Space Fashion

The garments worn by astronauts will become an important part of their identity, not just in terms of their functional support of the body, but as a decorative covering, like a new skin. As new fabrics and intelligent materials become incorporated into spacesuits, they will not just provide a reflection of aesthetic taste and culture, but form part of the adaptive and survival mechanisms for humans themselves.

Space Sports

Survival of the fittest in the extraterrestrial environment will be more appropriately rephrased as 'survival of the most adaptable', since the first pioneers, prior to natural genetic selection, will have to resort to the use of machines and artificial devices to survive. Space sports will exploit this competition between individuals and might be enacted at the Space Olympics. These commercial events would be extensively broadcast and would offer substantial prizes to winners, generating abundant advertising revenue for sponsors. Humans and machines would compete to achieve ground-breaking feats of speed, endurance and physical adeptness. Other sports could have a more military bias, taking the form of robotic gladiatorial contests. (There are already terrestrial versions of these pirate sports in Los Angeles, conducted by Mark Pauline's Survival Research Laboratories.)

Space Entertainment

Not only will space unify humans, it will perform the additional role of consolidating the relationship between technology and people, who will be inseparable from their machines. Space travellers will be dependent on their craft and on robot surveillance to patrol inhospitable environments.

Although humans will quickly adapt to the new orbital environments and the unique demands they place on the body, our gregarious instincts will be harder to appease. The isolation and loneliness of individually manned spacecraft will have to be addressed by interaction with the environment and with communications systems. Artificial intelligences will keep people company, and holographic entertainment will stimulate their imaginations. We will become socialised with virtual images of other humans, androids and automata. The entertainment industry will supply space travellers with regular programmes such as space-based soap operas or fantasy families with which to establish an ongoing relationship.

In order to reduce stress in the disoriented space traveller, music that samples and spontaneously composes itself could be a part of space architecture. This would disguise the perpetual hum of the power supply, which is capable of inducing psychological space sickness. Samples of the wind blowing, or the sound of the sea, may be woven into soundtrack samples to remind the space traveller or inhabitant of Earth. Remaining in touch with our human origins will be an essential part of space life.

Life and Death in Space

The mass communications networks will provide one of the first ways in which humans start to imagine what life might be like in space. With the establishment of an orbital tourist industry, people will not only begin to believe that it is possible to venture into orbit, but regard it as a right. As vacations into orbit become longer, the prospect of orbital habitation will appeal to some. This migration from the Earth will signify an important stage in human evolution as our capacity to thrive in these constructed environments will be defined by the limits of our physiology and genetics.

As orbital life is shown to have a place in human society, space will be seen as another terrain for both living and dying. Space burials will be cheaper than those on Earth and it may become popular to follow in the pathway of Star Trek visionary Gene Roddenberry with a celestial ceremony. In order to avoid the build-up of debris, there may even be designated space cemeteries for jettisoned corpses.

Pollution

Space debris is already a hazard in orbit, but as the number of visitors increases the ecology of our near orbits will need to be addressed. Space-cleansing operations should be designed to ensure that ships entering space do not collide with the rubbish that humans leave behind.

Conclusion

The concept of human habitation in space is, of course, a very old one; in some form, it can be traced back to the early days of science and even earlier, to mysticism. It has been a theme of fiction and speculation. This century has brought the first real access to extraterrestrial space and, with it, the architectural community is faced with the prospect of thinking the unthinkable about where we will live and the way in which we can best accomplish this. Δ

Notes
1 Gerard K O'Neill, The High Frontier: Human Colonies in Space, Corgi (London), 1977.

Biographies

⟁ Space Architecture

Dr Buzz Aldrin and Neil Armstrong were the first people to set foot on another planet in the Apollo XI Moon walk, 1969. Since retiring from NASA and the Air Force, he has remained at the forefront of space exploration. His autobiography appeared in 1974, and in 1996, he published his science-fiction novel, *Encounter With Tiber* . He is Chair of the National Space Society and the ShareSpace Foundation.

Dr Rachel Armstrong is a multimedia producer, medical doctor, lecturer, writer and broadcaster specialising in new technology and the arts. She is a presenter for the BBC's UK Arena programme 'The Frame', and for Sky Television's 'dot'. Her fiction work, *A Gray's Anatomy*, is published this year. scifi@dircon.co.uk

David Ashford is Managing Director of Bristol Spaceplanes Limited, whose major project is the Ascender sub-orbital spaceplane. He has worked as an aerodynamicist, project engineer and project manager on DC-8, DC-10, Concorde and the Skylark sounding rocket. He is co-author with Patrick Collins of *Your Spaceflight Manual – How You Could be a Tourist in Space Within Twenty Years* (1990). www.spacefuture.com

The Bartlett School of Architecture, Building, Environmental Design and Planning, part of the University of London, offers its 900 students a multidisciplinary approach to the study of the built environment. Internationally recognised as a centre of excellence for both research and teaching, it is at the forefront of architectural debate.

David Bowie is a singer, songwriter and performer who has constantly reinvented himself, from his alter egos Ziggy Stardust and the Thin White Duke, through his acting roles in Nic Roeg's *The Man Who Fell to Earth* (1976) and Nagisa Oshima's *Merry Christmas Mr Lawrence* (1982), to his latest incarnation as artist and art collector.

Esther De Angelis's computer collage compositions hybridise animal, mineral and vegetable forms to suggest terraformed environments, 'unnatural selection' and new, artificial worlds.

Dr Patrick Collins is a researcher at NASDA and Professor of Economics at Azabu University. His main subject of research is the commercialisation of space activities. He was consultant for ESA, a member of the Japanese SPS 2000 Task Team and Chairman of the Space Tourism Business Research Committee of the Japanese Rocket Society. www.spacefuture.com

Dr Peter H Diamandis is Chairman of the X-PRIZE Foundation , promoting the formation of a space-tourism industry through a $10,000,000 prize. The recipient of numerous awards, he is President of Angel Technologies Corporation, and founder of International MicroSpace, Inc; Constellation Communications, Inc and International Space University. His research includes molecular genetics, space medicine and launch vehicle design. www.xprize.org

Martyn Fogg is a science writer affiliated with the Probability Research Group, UK, and an internationally recognised research worker in the subject of terraforming. He has published widely on diverse aspects of astronomy and planetary science and acted as consultant for the BBC, NASA and the BIS. mfogg@globalnet.co.uk

Anders Hansson is the Founding Director of the European Institute of Quantum Computing, a full member of the International Astronautical Academy, consultant to Reaction Engines Ltd, and fellow of the British Interplanetary Society.

Edwin Heathcote is an architect and writer living in London. He writes on architecture for *The Financial Times* and several architectural journals. He is the editor of *Church Building* magazine and has written several books for Wiley-Academy including *Church Builders, Monument Builders, Bank Builders* and *Imre Makovecz: Wings of the Soul*. He is currently writing a book on cinema architecture and has contributed an essay on modernism to ⟁ *Architecture and Film II*.

Kazuyoshi Yajima is Vice Dean and Professor at the Department of Hygiene/Space Medicine, Nihon University. He is a Fellow of the Aerospace Medical Association (USA) and a special member of the Space Activity Commission of Japan. In 1993 he was awarded the Tsiolokovsky Medal from the Ministry of Health, Russia.

Ted Krueger is Director of Information Technology at the School of Architecture, University of Arkansas. He has exhibited, lectured and published on an international basis for more than a decade on topics related to the social and cultural implications of technology. tkrueger@comp.uark.edu

Suzanne Lee is Senior Lecturer for the MA Fashion/Textiles programme at the University of Central England, Birmingham and a member of digital art collective, Spore. She was consultant for the Hayward Gallery's *100 Years of Art & Fashion* exhibition and co-curator of *Lost and Found* for The British Council. suzanne@spore.co.uk

Robert T McCall has been the official space artist to NASA for more than thirty-five years. He was also employed as conceptual artist on major movies such as Stanley Kubrick's *2001: A Space Odyssey* (1968), the *Star Trek* movies and Disney's *The Black Hole* (1979).

Mathis Osterhage began training as an architect at the Fachhochschule Düsseldorf. He came to England in 1996 and completed his diploma at the Bartlett School of Architecture, where he is researching urban design. He has won various prizes including the 1997 RIBA bronze medal for architecture in education.

Rachel Rosenthal is an international performer, writer and teacher whose work centres around the issue of humanity's place on the planet. She has won numerous awards, including the OBIE, the Women's Caucus for the Arts Honor Award for Outstanding Achievement in the Arts and a career achievement award from *LA Weekly*.

Jason Skeet (Inner-City AAA) is part of the Association of Autonomous Astronauts' worldwide network of independent and community-based space exploration groups. jason@deepdisc.com

Richard Taylor is a British Airways B747-400 captain with 33 years flying experience. He is a member of the Space Frontier Foundation and The Royal Aeronautical Society and has contacts with NASA and the Rotary Rocket Company.

Thomas Taylor is a third-year student at the University of Bristol, UK, on a Physics MSc course. He is Chair of United Kingdom Students for the Exploration and Development of Space. He has also been involved in building a sounding rocket. tt7367@bristol.ac.uk

Simon Thorogood is a modern couturier whose work centres on challenging traditional contexts for fashion. He shows 'off-schedule', inviting collaboration in the presentation of his collections. He is also a fashion lecturer at Winchester School of Art. simon_thorogood@hotmail.com

Howard Wolff is Vice President and Corporate Managing Director of Wimberly Allison Tong & Goo, an international design and consulting practice specialising in leisure and entertainment. He is advisor to the Space Tourism Society and The Space Travel and Tourism Division of the Space Transportation Association. Hwolff@watg.com

Dr John Zukowsky is Curator of Architecture at the Art Institute of Chicago. His exhibitions and books include *Building for Air Travel: Architecture and Design for Commercial Aviation* (1996), *Building for Space Travel* (2001) and *Space Architecture: The Work of John Frassanito & Associates for NASA* (1999).

Popscene

In November 1999, Wiley-Academy published an important new book on the architecture of Mark Fisher, the designer of the Millennium Dome in Greenwich and some of the greatest pop stadia architecture since the 1960s. Bob Fear charts the shifting aesthetic values of the music performance space, including Zaha Hadid's recent stage sets for the Pet Shop Boys' world tour, and the impact of the pop video on the live event.

The music industry has a history of providing live events spectacular enough to match the egos of even the most flamboyant performers, from the iconic figures of Bowie and Hendrix in the 1970s, to the leather, hair and pyrotechnics of Heavy Metal and M-O-R Rock, to the limits of excess explored by U2 in the 1990s. Eric Holding's monograph on designer Mark Fisher chronicles the journey of the stadium rock concert, spanning the Beatles at Shea Stadium in 1965 and U2's Popmart in Las Vegas 30 years later, taking in on the way Fisher's gargantuan stage sets for Pink Floyd and the Rolling Stones. Holding provides a brilliant and unique perspective on the processes of bringing these epic projects to life. He also raises questions of selling-out to commercialism and rock'n'roll authenticity, concluding with the observation that increasing levels of excess (enacted, albeit with supposed irony, by U2) inevitably result in backlash.

This has certainly been the case. The Stones, Pink Floyd and U2 are no longer thought cool by the kids. As Holding points out, 'the rock spectacle is seen as part of the establishment against which a group needs to rebel in order to resist commodification'. We even cringe at the term 'rock' in this context, which would have to be delivered in a Smashey and Nicey voice to achieve the necessary level of irony. At a time when it's suddenly cool to like Steps and the Spice Girls, we're more comfortable with the term, 'pop'.

The aesthetics of the pop artists' performance space seem to be largely dictated by a principle of unchallenging compromise. After all, that is the essence of pop: it's a wide, all-accommodating middle-ground into which the splinters of the scene fall head-over-heels – epitomised by Cher being knocked off the number one spot by the equally compromising Offspring. Bland minimalism and functional signification of a band's identity courtesy of a token banner or lighting effect seem to suffice.

Even amongst steadfast, hardcore gig-goers a crisis arose two summers ago when the age of the music festival reached its peak. Just when the way forward seemed to be the all-day or weekend festival-in-a-field, the industry saturated us with a plethora of high-priced events, often featuring the same bands. Many groups became mere warm-ups for these events, their own tours down-sized and relegated to small venues due to poor ticket sales. One festival was cancelled because no-one had the money or the inclination to spend the whole summer herded into a field, their camera confiscated, having to fork out £3 for a pint in a sponsored plastic cup. The blind, greedy music-industry philosophy of 'bigger, better, faster, more' (as coined by the Manic Street Preachers) ate itself up again.

Holding quotes showdirector Willie Williams' observation that a saturation of spectacle has resulted in a 'greatly reduced sense of wonder' and widespread apathy. This is borne out by the most recent, large-scale, globe-spanning, stadium musical event, NetAid. Pale in comparison to Live Aid, its promise to deliver a world-changing event barely registered – presumably at the cost of charity donations whose newsworthiness would at least have provided a wake-up call to those controlling Third World debt. Perhaps it is also symptomatic of the failure of the Swiftian-scaled Millennium Dome to capture our imaginations and wallets?

So what does lie amidst the rubble left by Mark Fisher? Is there still a place on the stage for the frustrated pop-star that dwells within the architectural designer?

Holding acknowledges the shift in the music follower's aesthetic attention since the advent of the pop video, which came to prevalence in the 1980s, adding

> Although the 'image' of individual rock bands has been carefully controlled throughout the short history of this cultural phenomenon, the use of video has not only increased the frequency with which they are encountered visually, but also provides a powerful means by which this image can be controlled or constructed.

In such a fickle business, a fleeting moment of credibility, sought through the pop promo, is all that is needed to secure profit on massive corporate investment. The current structure of the music scene denies 'safe bets' – as the Stones and Pink Floyd once were. For if any band reaches such status, it immediately negates their credibility – as happened to Oasis. One minute they were bragging about the size of their Knebworth, the next they were pictured shopping with their 'rock-star wives' on the back pages of *Hello!*

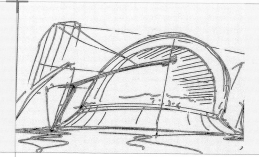

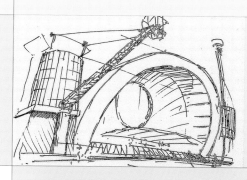

And nothing could so successfully alienate the discerning music fan as that.

The way back to credibility, if not through consistently brilliant and innovative music, may be via the 'breakthru' video, which warrants its own category in the MTV awards. A carefully constructed, 'perfect' performance space is designed for us to enjoy an ideal, intimate encounter with our favourite artist, where the sound and view are just right. Ironically, the key to the successful performance video seems to be its ability to appeal to our nostalgia for the perfect gig, without the discomfort and inconvenience, which we can easily avoid from the safety of our armchair.

Persuade us not to flick over to the cartoons and we might even consider booking a couple of tickets and risking the potential nightmare that is a trip to Wembley. But for many, the spectacle of the groovy-mover Jamiroquai bouncing around, anti-gravity-fashion in a virtually realised sci-fi set that contorts our concepts of real space and time, far outweighs the appeal of seeing a fidgety midget in a big hat on stage in the distance. In these lazy, waist-expanding days of ultra-convenience, film has largely replaced theatre as our preferred entertainment and perhaps has also slowly been replacing our need to see our favourite artists in the flesh.

When Pink Floyd and the Stones were earning their millions in front of an older generation of mulleted, die-hard musos in the world's stadiums, the pop video was gathering strength in the living room as the preferred method of worship. The first videos generally recreated the straight concert performance in unspectacular surroundings. Aside from the revolutionary Quantel effects pioneered in the promo for Queen's 'Bohemian Rhapsody', the rest of the video concentrated in the stunning attractiveness of the lycra-clad band on a bland, backdrop-free stage. Groups then realised that all the world was indeed their stage. Blondie ventured into the legendary Studio 54 for 'Heart of Glass' to give a fashionable context to their performance. The Village People imaginatively strutted their stuff on the streets outside the YMCA (cue camera zooming in on each letter in time with the chorus) and the Police washed up on a 'desert island' beach for 'Message In A Bottle'. All of these literal interpretations hardly ventured beyond the imaginations of Pan's People and their 'Top of the Pops' dance routine 'concepts' (memories of black and white stripes, face-masks and swag bags still haunt me every time I hear

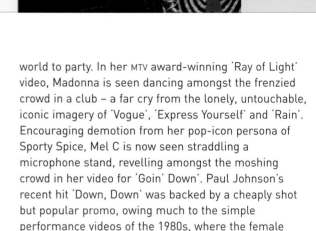

To create a live experience for their audience, REM use dramatic
abstract lighting and projections on to huge screens.

The Clash's 'Bankrobber'). The thing that most of these early performance videos have in common is their lack of audience, which somehow makes viewing them a cold and awkward experience (beyond any nostalgic feeling that they now conjure up). They merely offered convenience and novelty – surely nothing seriously to challenge the concert experience?

Bands such as the Boomtown Rats, Madness and Adam and the Ants pioneered a very British, semi-surreal approach that owed much to Monty Python. This involved lots of dream-like storytelling enacted by grotesque characters in bizarre situations. However progressive and innovative these promos may have been, they were still bound by real space, if not by real time. So when Madonna was still ducking bridges in Venice, proclaiming her born-again virginity, and Michael Jackson was encouraging early LA gang members in leg-warmers and head-bands to 'Beat It', the unlikely vehicles of pioneering design technology were A-HA, who introduced us to the fantasy story, where sketched characters on a page find a way to break through the boundary between their 2-D world and this. The 'real' woman looking over the storyboard is understandably surprised to find a sketched hand gain an extra dimension, reach out from the page and pull her into the black and white domain. Dire Straits utilised fledgling digital animation technology to bring us the defining 'Money For Nothing' promo, with its computer-generated characters, which revolutionised the standards by which MTV designated all-important airtime. Peter Gabriel never let the camera's gaze move from a simple head and shoulders shot for 'Sledgehammer', but the immediate surroundings transformed from rollercoaster ride to a surreal coop of dancing headless chickens.

This manipulation, distortion and exaggeration of real space in order to create fantastical performance arenas has fast-developed over the years to culminate in the digital chocolate world of Shanks and Bigfoot and the extremely complementary, Lara Croft-inspired renderings of the girls from the Venga Boys for last summer's Ibiza anthem. It has elevated the art of the video promo to an appealing level, way beyond the reach of the concert performance. The cleverer the video, the more credible the artist. This reliance is on the fantasy image created in the video may be seen as a necessity, however, when most of the new dance acts, such as the latter two artists, are mere, faceless DJs sampling simple beats, rhythms and lyric hooks; their actual physicality is not perhaps dynamic enough to rival other 'traditional' performers. The continuation of technological, television-bound advances that offer designers the chance to experiment with the potential of the performance space suggests that the static medium of the concert has indeed gone as far as it can.

It is interesting to note, however, that some artists are utilising the presence of a crowd in their videos, suggesting that there is indeed some credibility left in this notion of tearing ourselves away from the TV and joining the outside world to party. In her MTV award-winning 'Ray of Light' video, Madonna is seen dancing amongst the frenzied crowd in a club – a far cry from the lonely, untouchable, iconic imagery of 'Vogue', 'Express Yourself' and 'Rain'. Encouraging demotion from her pop-icon persona of Sporty Spice, Mel C is now seen straddling a microphone stand, revelling amongst the moshing crowd in her video for 'Goin' Down'. Paul Johnson's recent hit 'Down, Down' was backed by a cheaply shot but popular promo, owing much to the simple performance videos of the 1980s, where the female lead ventures down beneath a Mediterranean beach to find a blissful, happening club.

These simple concepts featuring a return to real space may be a reaction to the reliance on special effects, an effort to re-assert the authenticity of artists as 'live' performers. There is nothing outstanding in the design of the performance spaces in these films: they are in fact deliberately neutral, generic dance spaces. At a time when all types of dance music predominate in the charts, it is no longer the perfect gig that videos may wish to recreate, but the perfect night clubbing. It does seem that we would now rather throw ourselves into the hedonistic crowds at a club than at a gig. This could be due to the onslaught of drug and DJ culture, offering us a new way to let them entertain us.

But remnants of the nostalgic appeal of the perfect gig must still hold some promise for the future of the concert. Intermittently and successfully gigging artists such as REM and Bjork will still draw the crowds. REM ironically rely on the projection of film on huge screens, or simple yet abstract lighting designs – as seen on last year's short tour – to encourage their fans to attend. But their live, emotionally-charged rendition of 'Everybody Hurts' was a moving experience that would only work when amongst a large crowd. The reliably innovative Bjork continues to stretch boundaries in her concepts for gigs as well as music videos. Large, abstract creations and projections litter her performance space, but do not overwhelm it . By her sheer presence and the magnitude of her voice – exploring new renditions of her songs – she always remains the centre of attention. Both REM and Bjork offer something in their live events that cannot be experienced on the screen. And the sense of epic spectacle comes from the performers themselves, not the stage set. Here then, is the key to ensuring the continuation of the credible stadium gig – unique, perhaps improvisational performances that communicate on an emotional level. Of course, there will always be a successful concert when the performers are preaching to the converted; nothing

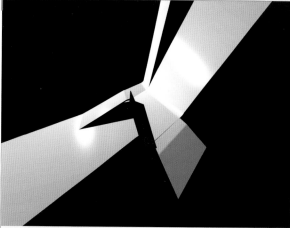

beats seeing your favourite band live when you've followed them for most of your life, which is perhaps how the Stones and Pink Floyd managed it.

Apart from the guaranteed money-spinning stadium fillers such as Boyzone and the Spice Girls, whose audiences only require token pyrotechnics and video screens to wow them, the Pet Shop Boys are now one of the few bands touring who still dare to try something new. The very fact that they are performing in front of large audiences is a departure, having initially declared their reluctance to do so. Their first tour was an attempt to utilise every visual stimuli, from video screens to dance troupes, to distract from their unspectacular physical presence. The music itself is largely superficial, sing-a-long synth-pop. A couple of years ago they staged another set of concerts offering a distinctly static, theatrical experience for the committed fan. Their rare forays onto the tour circuit now work in much the same way as those of the Stones and Pink Floyd: their career longevity, which appeals to a sense of nostalgia, ensures good ticket sales, as does the offer of hearing new work at a unique event. In no danger of over-exposure and saturation, they can afford to turn to a renowned designer to provide them with an interesting performance space.

Zaha Hadid's designs for the 1999 world tour craftily offer an apparently simplistic, white structure, which metamorphoses with each number, offering a continually changing and cleverly diverse performance space. As project architect Oliver Domeisen says:

> Rather than composing spatial sequences, we unfold a white canvas that contains and directs the dynamics of a pop concert. A single continuous surface is thrown into relief as it bends and splits to create background, structure and floor. Other parts of this surface become detachable, mobile elements that act as choreographic tools on a three-dimensional luminous landscape of projection and sound.

Hadid and her team have produced a relatively minimal stage set in comparison to Fisher's works. It's appeal lies in its sleek simplicity. It manages to perform the function of spectacle without resorting to excesses; it is easily transportable to each venue, and enhances rather than dwarfs or distracts from Tennant and Lowe and their four-man dance troupe. This performance space gives us reason to head into the madding crowds and witness something we can't see at home – which is exactly where we can leave our over-exposed-rock-star-weary cynicism. ⚫

Eric Holding, *Mark Fisher: Stage Architecture*, is published by Wiley-Academy and costs £24.95 ($45).

Jan Stratford

An Overview of Architectural Design 1930–1977

The Ideas Circus

The △D logo, originally designed by Adrian George, built out of driftwood in Berkeley, California. Constructed by Peter Murray, Brian Mitchenere, Kathy de Witt and Suzanne Growhurst.

This year, *Architectural Design* is celebrating its 70th anniversary. To mark the occasion, △D Plus will run a series on the history of the journal with contributions from many of those previously on its editorial staff, who most notably include Kenneth Frampton, Robin Middleton, Peter Murray, Martin Spring and Haig Beck; there will also be an article by Charles Jencks, △D's prestigious and longest standing contributor. As a preface to the series, we present an overview of △D's formative period, 1930–1977, when it developed from an advertising supplement into a publication espousing architecture's most cutting-edge ideas. Researched by Jan Stratford as part of a postgraduate thesis, the article has been compiled with the aid of Monica Pidgeon, △D's influential and long-serving Editor (1946–1975), who in 1999 received an honorary doctorate from the Architectural Association in London for her considerable contribution to architecture.

△ December 1953 △ November 1955 △ January 1957 △ June 1962

The covers designed by Theo Crosy between December 1953 and June 1962, while he was Technical Editor at △, were some of the finest ever produced for the magazine. Afterwards Crosby went on to found the British design company Pentagram.

Over the years, *Architectural Design*'s history has been one of incremental and steady evolution. As a result, after decades of continuous change, it bears little resemblance to its earliest incarnations in the 1930s. Having started out as a small-scale publication supported by advertising, it has developed into an international subscription journal with the production qualities of a book rather than a news stand magazine. Though by 1945 it had been going for some 15 years, it only really came to the fore in the post-war period, when Monica Pidgeon was at the helm. △'s accession was largely due to its ability to be responsive both to shifts in publishing and in the architectural scene. Pidgeon recounts the changes in printing techniques over these years, and the changes in format that they afforded, as well as the influential architects with whom she worked. Above all, she acknowledges the creative individuals who were employed with her on the magazine's staff.

The journal's origins lie in a 'building centre' that was started up in November 1930 by three architects in a basement at 26 Bloomsbury Way, London. The centre was rapidly superseded by a printed publication, which resulted in the Architect's Standard Catalogue. This was given away free to 4,000 architectural practices, each page being paid for by advertising. It was not until 1932, however, that the name 'Architectural Design' first emerged, when the Architect's Standard Catalogue was brought with an accompanying journal called *Architectural Design and Construction*. This was also complimentary, all the production costs being covered by advertising. It contained light-hearted articles on contemporary artists and architects.

The first Editor of the journal was a man named Kendall, but it remained very much in its infant stages until FE Towndrow took it over in 1932. Up until this time, Towndrow had been writing 'fill-in' articles at short notice, when copy from other contributors did not arrive in time for printing. Under Towndrow's editorship, a balance was created in the journal between critical and philosophical discussion. As a consequence, *AD&C* now included detailed descriptions of the latest buildings, news features on professional topics, and reviews of new materials and building methods, as well as travel articles and essays of aesthetic or scholarly interest.

Inevitably, the war forced changes on the staff at the journal. In 1942, Towndrow was appointed Director of the Ministry of Works at Lambeth Bridge House. He responded to the problem of editing the magazine in absentia by asking Pidgeon, who had done occasional work for *AD&C* and studied architecture at the Bartlett in London, to ghost for him. For the rest of the war, she and Barbara Randell, Towndrow's secretary, operated the journal under his overall direction. Each month, they would take the draft copy to show him, and then, when he had given it his approval, they would take it to the company's own printers, the Whitefriars Press in Tonbridge, Kent. It was only in 1945, when the war was ended, and Towndrow was offered the post of Dean of the Faculty of Architecture and Building at the new South Wales Technical University in Sydney, that Pidgeon, who now had plenty of experience editing △, took over as joint editor with Barbara Randell.

Already, by the January 1946 issue, a number of significant changes were in place that were to bring about the popular format of the 1950s and 1960s: the magazine was renamed *Architectural Design* and the number of pages was increased to 30. By June 1946, a single colour had been introduced. The inclusion of colour was a very gradual process, which did not truly get underway until the early 1950s when more than one colour could be applied. Even then, colour printing remained expensive, as the magazine was printed by a letter press. The distribution of colour was limited to sections of the journal where it had been paid for by advertising; these sections did not relate to the running order, but to the magazine sheets, which were cut down and folded to make pages. The editors therefore had to be entirely opportunistic in their use of the colour blocks, planning page allocation around adverts.

Though a key architectural magazine of the 1950s, △'s circulation continued to be small in relation to the other architectural journals of the time. It was intentionally aimed by Pidgeon at young architects and students because, as she now states, 'they were the future of architecture, open to new ideas!'[1] Run on a tight budget, it did not hope to compete in terms of production and new photography with other publications such as *Architectural Review*, which tended to be regarded as the luxury architectural magazine and *The Architects' Journal*, a 'mid-range' publication. △ catered for its young readership with features on art and new buildings, including more practical technical articles, such as brick dimension tables and a series of basic introductory pieces on drainage and plumbing.

In July 1952, the design and colour of the front cover were altered. This was a major breakthrough: until

The vibrancy and spontaneous energy of *D*'s covers and scrapbook-like inside pages in the late 60s and early 70s reflected its avant-garde stance and the excitement that it created on the architectural scene.

then, the rather drab cover had been a uniform maroon colour every month, with a large advertisement for the British Constructional Steelwork Association as the focal point. From this point on, Theo Crosby designed some of the most beautiful covers in *D*'s history, which can be considered works of art. Crosby had joined *Architectural Design* in 1953 in the newly created position of 'Technical Editor', when Barbara Randell left to start a family.

By the mid to late 1950s, *D* was beginning to establish itself as the promoter of architects and writers whose ideas did not fit in with the national Contemporary style, advocated in the immediate post-war years by professional institutions, most notably by the LCC Housing Department, and *The Architectural Review*. Crosby summed up the attitude of more forward-looking architectural thinkers: 'When I hear the word Contemporary, I reach for my revolver.'[2]

D became a magnet for those such as Cedric Price and Archigram, who were effectively snubbed by the RIBA and the establishment for their anti-style and non-conformist ideas. *D* shared their enthusiasm for the future – energy, space travel, communications and computer technology. More than any other architectural publication, it reflected the exciting and progressive milieu centred on the AA and the ICA in London.

After nine years as Technical Editor, Crosby, who, as an active member of the Independent Group, had injected his passionate ideas into the journal, left *D*. The position of Technical Editor was filled by Kenneth Frampton. Now Ware Professor at the Graduate School of Architecture and Planning, Columbia University, Frampton is best known for writing a seminal history of 20th-century architecture, *Modern Architecture: A Critical History*. Pidgeon, who describes him as a highly meticulous person, credits him with having brought a more serious look to the magazine at this time.

After two years, Frampton left *D*, in 1964, to go to Princeton, and was replaced by Robin Middleton, an eminent art historian who specialised in Ledoux's work. Pidgeon and Middleton worked well together and all the changes to *D* that happened subsequently were decided jointly.[3] By the end of the 1960s and beginning of the 1970s, the journal had grown in popularity and the number of subscribers had increased. *D*'s subject matter had become thoroughly enmeshed in the pop culture of the decade. Cover designs became dominated by psychedelic colours and patterns, and inside, technology and the future predominated.

Peter Murray, who joined the magazine in 1969 as Art Editor, took over as Technical Editor when Middleton left.

At this time, Adrian George designed the new logo, which has provided the model for its redesign in 2000. Still the journal could not attempt to present buildings in a large format with glossy colours, as the quality of the paper would not withstand such printing. Instead, the focus remained on bright blocks of colour mingled with text, and an abundance of line drawings. Murray remembers that many of the articles were 'collaged' together from other architectural magazines, which gave *D* a 'scrap book feel'.[4] The office hours were unconventional – 11 am to 7 pm – and the staff worked around one large table stacked with papers.

In 1973, Murray left the journal to become editor of *Building Design*. Two years later, in November 1975, Pidgeon resigned to take up a new post as Editor of the RIBA *Journal*. She was replaced by Martin Spring, with Haig Beck as Associate Editor.

The magazine was still not making a profit, but it was covering its production costs. As soon as Pidgeon declared her intention to leave, the Standard Catalogue Company approached United Trade Press who wanted to buy it, complete with editorial staff. Spring and Beck refused, and in May 1976 bought the magazine from the parent company and began to run it as their own independent company called Acroshaw Limited. Later, Dr Andreas Papadakis took over as Publisher. This meant a move to new premises at 7/8 Holland Street, London.

The January 1977 issue of *D* shows a sudden improvement in paper quality – a smooth, shiny, expensive paper, never before used in the journal. When, in April 1977, Martin Spring left the journal, it had already begun to take on a new format, characteristic of later issues, when Papadakis took over as Editor. In the May 1977 edition, Papadakis is listed as Publisher and Haig Beck as Editor. Following this, the journal began to be published bi-monthly and the cover price increased. Haig Beck stayed with the journal until June 1979, after which Papadakis took the role of Editor as well as Publisher.

Under Papadakis, *D* was reinvented for a new audience of architects worldwide. It was no longer produced with students and young architects in mind. The magazine was printed on the very best paper in a larger format with glossy illustrations. Papadakis held a regular series of conferences and lectures to

which he invited the newly emerging architectural stars on the international circuit. These provided him with the material for the magazine. Just as *Δ* had captured the spirit of the times in the previous decades, Papadakis put the journal at the centre of debates in architecture, covering every mutation of style and trend, including Postmodernism, Classicism and Deconstruction. He also created *Δ Profiles* and *Art and Design*, among others, selling them on at the price of a hard-back book rather than a magazine.

In the middle years of the 20th century, *Δ* established itself as a platform, or an 'ideas circus', from which new and challenging notions could be displayed, discussed and considered in detail. Often, the writers and architects involved, in the 1950s and early 1960s at least, could not display their work through the usual channels, as their ideas were considered controversial or 'over the top'. The architecture and theories published in *Δ* were welcomed by receptive readers. Articles such as 'The Architectural Relevance of Cybernetics' (Gordon Pask), 'Sophisticated Versus Naive Methodological Falsification' (Imre Lakatos) and the psychedelic theories and accompanying colours of 'The Future is NOW!' all point to an audience of students with a propensity towards the new, the obscure and the potentially relevant, plus an eagerness and preparedness for the future.[5] *Δ*

Notes
1. Jan Stratford interviewing Monica Pidgeon, 5 June 1998.
2. *Architectural Design*, January 1955, anon, p 1.
3. Jan Stratford interviewing Peter Murray, 21 September 1998
4. Ibid.
5. *Architectural Design*, 1969.

Clare Design

Queensland, Australia, may seem an unlikely setting for developing the design tenets of a northern European modernist, but as editors of UME magazine, Haig Beck and Jackie Cooper found out, Lindsay and Kerry Clare of Clare Design have used the designs of Alvar Aalto as a starting point for the evolution of their own work — marked by its clarity and sensitivity to the environment.

Clare Residence, Buderim, Queensland, 1991

Above
South east elevation

Left
North east corner

During their 20 years' practice on Queensland's Sunshine Coast, north of Brisbane, Lindsay and Kerry Clare have established a supremely pragmatic response to the lush subtropical climate, undulating topography and easygoing holiday lifestyle. Their deceptively plain, elegant design signature is a product of their pared-down approach. Nothing extraneous or gratuitous is entertained.

Their main influence is Alvar Aalto, whose buildings they have made the pilgrimage to experience for themselves. Initially, as students, they were intrigued by the mystery suggested in Aalto's work; years of study have revealed the subtleties of his buildings' relationships to culture, tradition, living patterns, climate, geography. These lessons are all present in their own work. Another important influence has been local architect, Gabriel Poole. His work shows how architecture can be simultaneously modern and vernacular.

The Clares base their architecture on the objective of recreating experiences: the feeling of sitting in an open space behind a slatted or screened verandah, enjoying containment, comfort and breeze; of being on an elevated platform; or of sitting on the stairs as a breeze wafts through. They take the view that it is preferable to be connected to the environment rather than sealed off from it.

Queensland has a strong tradition of ample timber houses built on stilts, with wide verandahs. In the past 30 years, this timber vernacular has been sidelined by developers' brick veneer, which must be air-conditioned to cope with the heat in summer. The Clare's buildings do not rely on air-conditioning: summer temperatures inside the main spaces typically fall below ambient shaded temperatures outside. A lightweight building can achieve the same thermal benefits as heavy masonry construction.

Lightweight construction techniques are additive, and produce an additive aesthetic. Rather than attempting a seamless appearance, the architects express the way in which elements are assembled, Lego-like, taking pleasure in how things are layered and fixed. Textures produced with different materials help delineate intentions and explain spaces. The Clares have also developed an aesthetic that exposes the materials, which are left natural and self-finished wherever possible. They employ local hardwoods, leaving the grain exposed. The use of paint is restricted.

Fragmentation is inherent in the way they approach design. There cannot be a simple elevational treatment. Elements are separated and pulled apart. Joinery is often separated from walls. You see the space around things and transparency is sought. They enjoy combining and articulating materials: metal inlays in timber, for instance.

The plan is generally diagonal or axial, often fragmented to get light deep into the building and to improve ventilation. Balconies and decks are not tacked on but remain integral, linking internal spaces to the solitude of the landscape or the life of the street, pulling the outside inside. These elements are integral to the experience of being in a particular place.

The form of the roof serves both functional and expressive or poetic needs. The Clares often use skillion roofs, which echo the surrounding skillion and hipped roof forms of local vernacular buildings. The curved roof form is not their first choice, being too homogeneous, but is cheaper; they have used it on both their own house and on their pilot housing project, Cotton Tree.

The Clare's method is pragmatic, and their objective is economy – of effort, materials, resources. But this is the economy of perfectionists: everything requires careful detailing. Yet details, once refined, can be recycled from building to building. The Clares have rationalised these, limiting the number, with the result that a full spec can be completed in a few days. The same principles apply to a kitchen, whether it costs A$20,000 or A$3,000. Their cabinet-work drawings are poems to minimalism, describing only barely what is necessary: the result to be obtained, not how the joiner is to achieve it.

You would think perhaps that here is a design practice that has established a series of prescriptions, rules of thumb, to aid design, reducing it to a series of formulaic tactics. But the Clares practise a highly sophisticated type of modernism, which depends for its expression on several key ideas. These include an interest in the aestheticisation of fabrication and in minimalism. Minimalism is a 20th-century modernist notion that comes from the idea of abstraction. The expression of fabrication too is a modernist idea: it comes from opposition to a classical expression of tectonics. During 2,000 years of masonry construction and classical detailing, the building has been expressed as a homogeneous entity. Modernism, with its ideas of mass production in the machine age, introduced expression of a building's layered elements, showing fragmentation and the heterogeneous assembly of parts.

The Clares express the idea of a tectonic way of building. One appreciates the formal elements of architecture – roof, post, wall, window, floor, screen. These are all clearly expressed so that one can understand how things stand up and resist gravity. In particular, they give powerful expression to load-bearing elements: the post, the wall, the strut, the brace.

This approach springs in part from the local conditions, especially the vernacular construction techniques, which are lightweight and timber-framed. It also results from the need to respond to the hilly topography. While Cotton Tree sits on a flat, sandy flood-plain. a few hundred metres in behind the beach, other buildings by Clare Design are generally perched on precipitous rainforest slopes.

Also strongly evident in their work are ideas about a natural way of building and using natural techniques for dealing with climate, which serves to draw the user into a direct engagement with the place.

This is an architecture of critical regionalism. ◬

Haig Beck is a former editor of *Architectural Design*. He and Jackie Cooper live in Melbourne where they edit UME, an international review of architecture.

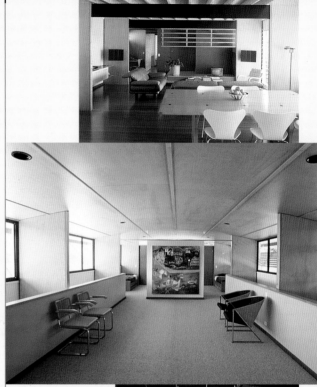

This speculative house provides a model for a cheap alternative to the fully tailor-made house. To achieve low construction costs, the structure was conceived of a two-storey timber box, framed and braced by plywood 'fin' walls along the perimeter. These fins also form alcoves along the perimeter, which create useful areas for entry, storage and work spaces. No internal walls are required for bracing or load bearing. This allows a high degree of flexibility to the interior spaces and the placement of services.

The house is sited across the contours to allow the full-width spaces to take maximum advantage of the landscape, sea views and the north-east aspect. The lower level has open-plan living areas, with the staircase and bathroom positioned to create a separate bedroom/study space. Children's bedrooms and play areas are on the upper level in contained, loft-like spaces.

The external cladding of corrugated sheet steel is scaled by deep louvre-window recesses in the wall and by a continuous band of glazing to the upper floor. The street elevation has a combination of metal louvres and battened eave struts for sun control, privacy and breeze penetration. The north-east elevation is quite private, allowing the house to open to the views and the land with glass louvres and swing doors.

Internally, the expression of the portal system provides a cohesive order through the length of the building, although the five bays vary in width according to the programme. The experience of the space entails a strong combination of both the tectonic and the tactile. For example, the living, dining and kitchen spaces are combined, yet delineated by various devices: fin walls, colour, the platform step and the expression of beams, reflected by floor insets of hoop pine. The plywood stairs, timber screen and built-in ply furniture blur the living room edge, yet give definition to spaces that are simultaneously drawn together by the ceiling and wall planes, materials and colours.

Fibre-cement sheeting gave flexibility. The east and west walls are brightly coloured to contrast with the corrugated metal sheeting. Plywood was used extensively as a structural element to brace walls and ceiling planes, and also for an attractive, workable internal lining.

The vertical connection between floor levels, achieved by voids and an open stair, allows air movement and balanced natural light to interior spaces. The voids have a secondary function, which is to foster a sense of community rather than separateness. For their own family, the architects wanted to engender a co-operative ethos through the relationships of spaces and the hierarchy of zones, without denying suitable degrees of privacy.

The house is a loose-fit skeletal structure that can be clad and subdivided according to site, programme and materials. It can be adapted to suit individual needs and the changing requirements of a growing family.

Top
View of living room

Middle
View of upstairs

Bottom
Entry deck

Below
North east
elevation at dusk

The University Club, University of the Sunshine Coast, Queensland, 1997

On a new university campus, this utilitarian building has the modest task of being sports pavilion, staff club and sometime classroom, a place for staff and students to mingle. The university initially considered putting up an industrial shed. Instead, Lindsay and Kerry Clare were commissioned to complete a building with 12 weeks construction time for some A$600,000. They had a bare six weeks for design, documentation and tendering.

The pavilion sits isolated in a vast area of grass, between two playing fields and straddling a drainage ditch. The modular, cross-sectional design lends itself to further extrusion, and the building can be extended lengthways in either direction, one of the requirements for flexibility.

Its east–west orientation is not ideal, but various tactics ensure effective passive climate control, despite the tropical weather extremes. The L-shaped deck sucks in air and provides ample, deep-shaded space. A gap in the roof draws in north light during winter and promotes a Venturi effect. It also breaks down the scale of roof elements. Louvres provide good cross-ventilation even when the sliding glazed doors must be closed against downpours and wind.

The exterior glazing needs hefty bracing for cyclone loadings. Bracing the edges of the building would compromise visibility from inside, so bracing is located in the centre instead, through trusses and big posts. The truss follows the arc of the verandah roofs. The building was required to be transparent on three sides, and the views from the interior of the Mooloolah Plain provide a dramatic horizontal panorama.

The emphatic horizontality is conscious, as much a response to the flat, expansive site as to the programme and the need for possible future extension. The challenge on such a long elevation is to fine down the edges. Walkway decks along the north-south sides of the building are formed as a two-tiered step that fines down the building edge along the ground line and enables people to sit on the floor with their feet on the verandah. At either end, the floating beams project to fine down the roof. Protruding 900 millimetres, they give an idea of telescoping, extendibility and ultimately definition to the end of the roof, creating a staccato of light/shade flickering rhythms. This rhythm is also produced along the ground edges, where unconcealed joists are visible below the flooring, and the constructional expression of the building also becomes its decoration. This has a very Queensland resonance and makes direct reference to the local vernacular of unlined timber buildings.

The roof is brought down low on the east and west sides to minimise the apertures and balance the light. The height of the roof (approximately 5 metres) is dictated by the need for efficient ventilation. The idea of the roof is that it is so light, it is propped. It floats, hovering unsupported, like an awning. All the support is in the centre.

Top
Interior detail
looking north

Middle
Interior showing
main space

Bottom left
Interior view
of servery

Bottom right
North west detail

Below
North elevation

Cotton Tree is a pilot housing prototype for affordable units that are environmentally, socially and aesthetically appropriate to this semi-tropical region. Built on two adjacent blocks, the development includes a mix of attached and detached, public and private dwellings, built around existing trees, with paved courts and covered parking.

The architecture reinterprets the planning, spatial and elevational treatments of the region's early beach houses, using light materials instead of the brick veneer and concrete roof tiles that have become the vernacular for speculative housing throughout Australia. Generally, a weatherproofing skin of masonry is used over an insulated timber frame. Here, however, the Clares take the insulating characteristics of masonry and put them on the inside, weatherproofing the building with a lightweight skin of corrugated iron and reinforced-fibre cement board. This inversion provides much more efficient insulation. Where conventional brick veneer encases the building as a homogeneous whole, reverse veneer expresses it as an assembly of parts. And while ubiquitous brick veneer cannot speak of place, the corrugated iron and cement-board are direct references to the lightweight coastal holiday-home vernacular.

By juxtaposing these two claddings, the Clares establish a scaling device that has references to rustication and ideas of a piano nobile, breaking down the three-storey building, superficially, into two storeys. The corrugated iron gives the expression of mass. An elegant, flimsy cement-board third storey, with its flyaway corrugated iron roof, is perched on top.

A main objective has been to avoid the image of public housing. For marketing purposes, the private development required townhouses on individual sites with party walls. A range of different household structures are satisfied. The public housing component is necessarily built to a greater density.

It is evident from the plans that Cotton Tree is a consummate exercise in different housing typologies. Each type is selected to suit the social or marketing agendas, and at the same time to preserve the trees on the site. Δ

Above top
North elevation
detail private housing

Above bottom
Entry detail

Left
South elevation
public housing

Clockwise from top left
South elevation detail
showing pedestrian
entry; south elevation
showing vehicle entry;
stair breezeway in private
housing; detail; north
elevation public housing

Clare DESIGN

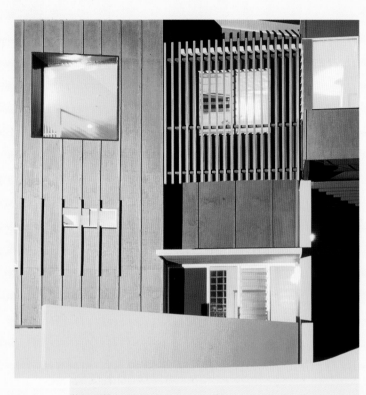

Above and below
South elevation

Biographical details

1979   Started up a practice on the Sunshine
        Coast together following graduation from
        Queensland University of Technology.

1991   Exhibited at the Venice Biennale

1992   Received the National Robin Boyd Award

1993   Received the National BHP Steel Futures
        Award

1994   Commissioned by the NSW State
        Government to prepare Livability paper

1995   Received the National Robin Boyd Award
        and the National RAIA Commercial Award

1996   Received the National RAIA Environment
        Citation and exhibited at the Milan Triennale

1998   Appointed Design Directors to the NSW
        Government Architect

1999   Appointed Adjunct Professors, Faculty
        of Architecture, University of Sydney

2000   Exhibited '10 Shades of Green' –
        The Architectural League of New York

Major Works

1984   Maroochy South Post Office

1989   Buderim War Memorial Hall Recycling

1991   Rainbow Shores 'Surfside'
        Attached Housing

1994   Hammond Residence

1995   Ski +Skurf Cable Ski Kiosk at Bli Bli

1997   Two Houses at Noosa

1999   National Environment Centre,
        Thurgoona Campus

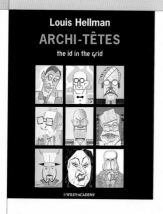

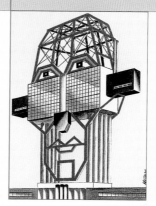

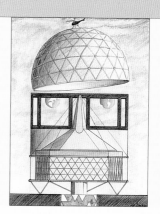

Those who believe that you will never see a big man walking a poodle, nor a little man with a St Bernard will have no problem with Louis Hellman's suggestion in his book of caricatures, *Archi-têtes*, that 'architects are the buildings they design'. He illustrates this theory with great verve, as the faces behind the big architectural names of the century metamorphose into their most characteristic creations.

The idea is such a good one that it is surprising it has not been done before. Hellman acknowledges the anthropomorphic portraits of Arcimboldo and the Surrealists by way of generic pedigree. However, by incorporating the works of his sitters into their portraits, he is able to offer a particularly revealing critique both of their buildings and of their characters. Thus, the primly austere features of Mies van der Rohe transform into a rigidly symmetrical design, whilst Gaudí's cavernous eye sockets and generous beard turn into an archi-tête that suggests both decorative exuberance and mystical withdrawal.

Within the artform he has created, Hellman is also able to sneak in the architects' particular trademarks. These can either be personal – a hint of Alvar Aalto's boozing, Le Corbusier's pipe, Frank Lloyd Wright's dandified attire – or professional: Dömenig has a metallic pterodactyl on his shoulder; Richard Rogers a crane.

The overall tone is one of irreverence tempered with an affectionate familiarity. Hellman's character notes, which introduce each archi-tête, reinforce this impression, with (sometimes rather laboured) limericks or clerihews, wry potted biographies and generally spot-on summaries of his victims' physical attributes. However some of his targets receive stronger treatment, the bonus non-architects, for instance, in the book (Tony Blair, Prince Charles, Ronald Reagan and Margaret Thatcher) afford Hellman the opportunity for visual polemics. The Prince of Wales, resembling nothing so much as an unloved piece of funerary architecture with the clock stopped at 1948, brings out Hellman at his most scathing.

Whilst one wouldn't want to belittle the invention that has gone into this book, a mischievous question suggests itself. Is Hellman lucky to find so many architects – not to mention a handful of furniture designers – whose features actually do resemble their creations? Or is something more spookily deterministic at work? Once presented with a photograph of the architect, it becomes hard to imagine that he could look any other way. One expects the creator of the Guggenheim museum in Bilbao to be curvaceous; the creator of the Hong Kong and Shanghai Bank to be exceptionally tall, athletic and somewhat forbidding in appearance. If Lutyens were as cadaverous as Voysey, Voysey as rotund as Lutyens, would their architectural styles be reversed? It is not entirely a facetious question, insofar as – and any caricaturist will tell you this – personal appearance cannot fail to have a bearing on character, and character cannot fail to have a bearing on creative production.

To take this reductionism one step further, it is evident that the period in which one lives exerts a culturally deterministic pressure, both on one's physical appearance and on the artifacts one produces. Baroque architects, wearing frilly collars and overflowing wigs, designed plumply ornate buildings. Neo-classical architects, wearing severe little powdered wigs, designed austere buildings. Victorian architects sported luxuriant quasi-Elizabethan beards and designed accordingly. After all, aren't the buildings we inhabit simply a looser form of clothing? The recognisably 20th-century photographs of the architects that accompany Hellman's text morph elegantly into distinctly 20th-century caricature buildings. It would be fascinating to see what a book of archi-têtes would look like 100 years hence.

In the meantime, viewing the world through Louis Hellman's eyes will allow us to make some short-term predictions: if Norman Foster develops a paunch, or Frank Gehry has his hair cropped, expect the unexpected. *Ð*

Archi-têtes: The Id in the Grid by Louis Hellman was published by Wiley-Academy (London) in 1999.

David Lewis is a cartoonist and caricaturist. He designed the cover for the Millennium Architecture issue of *Architectural Design*.

Bank Builder Edwin Heathcote
HB 0 471 85359 3; 305 x 252 mm; 224 pages;
February 2000

*Building Ideas: An Introduction to Architectural
Theory* Jonathan Hale PB 0 471 85194 9;
229 x 152 mm; 256 pages; March 2000

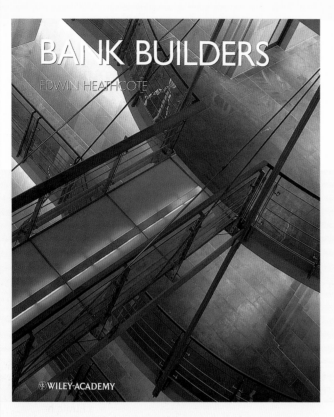

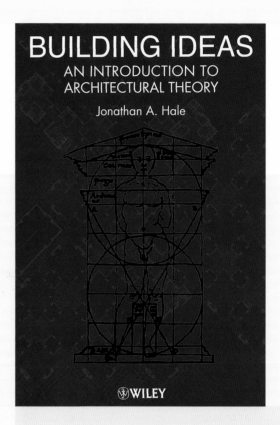

Despite their often conservative image, banks and financial corporations have been responsible for commissioning some of the most interesting and innovative modern architecture, as architects have responded to the challenge of designing a building that is both welcoming and highly secure. Following in the successful 'Builders' series, which includes titles on museums, theatres, churches, libraries, monuments and airports, this book monitors the broad spectrum of design in the banking field throughout the world. In an introductory essay, Heathcote examines the roots of the architecture of banking – from early money-changers' stalls, through the Florentine Renaissance palaces of financial commerce and the later works of Sir John Soane, Otto Wagner, Louis Sullivan and others, to the most radical recent examples, discussing the implications for building in the next millennium. A series of richly illustrated sections on notable contemporary bank buildings – including Foster Associates' Hong Kong and Shanghai Bank in Hong Kong, Frank O Gehry's DG Bank in Berlin, Cesar Pelli's Norwest Center in Minneapolis, Odile Decq and Benoit Cornette's Banque Populaire de L'Ouest in Rennes and a myriad of others – proves that there is room for stylistic diversity even in this most established of building types. ⅅ

Answering the huge demand for a clear introduction to the major theoretical debates in architecture, *Building Ideas* introduces and discusses selected contemporary approaches to architectural theory, analysis and criticism. Its author, Jonathan Hale, has an excellent reputation as a lecturer who communicates architectural theories to his students in a direct, clear and comprehensive manner, and his highly accessible style of writing enables a wider audience to understand the concepts behind this often bewildering field. Each chapter deals with a specific approach by presenting a range of related buildings as illustrations of a key theoretical position, as well as setting this position in a cultural and historical context. Providing the theoretical tools necessary for an understanding of the history of philosophies and technologies in architecture, this book is essential reading for undergraduate architectural theory courses, as well as a first point of reference for anyone wishing to comprehend the complex connections between architectural practice and related fields of cultural enquiry. It also acts as a guide and companion volume to the many primary theoretical texts recently made available in reprinted collections. ⅅ

Book Review

Katherine MacInnes, who was appointed Senior Commissioning Editor at Architectural Press in Spring 1999, takes a look at two books that were published last year.

Sustainable Practices: ESD and the Construction Industry, edited by Craig Langston, Environbook(Sydney), 1997, and Jon Carpenter Publishing (Charlbury, Oxfordshire), 1999, 243pp, b/w, PB £12.00

Nigel Coates: Body Buildings and City Scapes by Jonathan Glancey, Thames and Hudson (London), 1999, 150 colour photos, HB £9.95

You may not be able to tell a book by its cover but with *Sustainable Practices* the tight type face, spare margins and recycled paper are a give away – a refreshing example of a book that literally practices what it preaches.

The 24 refereed papers that make up this title analyse ESD 'ecologically sustainable development' from a wide variety of angles. In an attempt to overcome the usual problem of combining a disparate set of essays – each paper is organised in progression from macro to micro issues.

This allows the book to appeal both the environmental professional for whom words like 'phytoplankton' are common currency and the lay-reader who will be interested to know that the ozone layer 'is a layer of pale blue gas located in the stratosphere occupying an altitude of about 15km up to 50km above the Earth's surface'.

As Craig Langston steers the book in relation to human economic activity – the reader is taken from Environmental Quality to Design considerations and from Project Feasibility studies through to Asset Management. In an area which is commonly given to speculation and drama – this book offers a cool, sometimes rather calculating look at practical and essential solutions. It strategic plans in the final chapter of the book should be given careful thought by the Construction industry.

It would have been useful to waste a bit of ink on some graphics to illustrate some of the points and a collated biography rather than the chapter specific version supplied would be useful in the future. Overall this is an essential 'how to' guide – how to practice in a sustainable, responsible way and one that is well worth £12.99. ⌂

It is obvious from his work that Coates 'never really thought of architecture as a good steady job so much as a pleasure, a way of life'. Glancey describes the dismissive criticism of James Stirling and Edward Jones who regarded Coates Unit 10 at he AA as 'the seed of a fresh approach to their jealously guarded discipline'. Coates describes his work as 'identified by its playful qualities, by accumulation and contradiction, by the overlaying of the extraordinary and the common place, by artistic intervention, by a filmic handling of space'. Thus rejecting what Glancey sees as the 'sterile language of functional compartments dressed in architectural clothes of this style or that'.

The book is a beautifully designed object in itself. A white jacketed hardback with transparent endpapers covered in Coates handwritten notes through which he rejects the distance of the book as a mass-produced product and achieves an intimacy that is his signature.

Even the Branson-Coates spin on the Dome is interesting – numbed as we have become to the constant drip, drip of Dome development – the Body Zone for which Branson Coates have designed a vast sculpture which is a building and exhibition space in its own right takes on a new resonance as we see its development inspired through ancient Etruscan modeling and the massive Soviet sculptures through Moore like sketches into its present form.

Jonathan Glancey's light chatty writing style suits this subject perfectly. Coates is a design wit. A self-styled agent provocateur with a rather extraordinary knack of being accepted and even identified with the Establishment with a capital 'E'. But then Coates would probably pass this off as just one more dynamic contradiction. ⌂

ACV-6416
39.9
2/22/01

Site Lines Carl Larsson House

Architectural historian Wendy
Hitchmough shows how Carl Larsson
used the medium of watercolour to
idealise his own domestic architecture
and publicise his work.

Carl Larsson,
The Kitchen from
'A Home' series
(watercolour
on paper),
c. 1865, in the
Nationalmuseum,
Stockholm.

Carl Larsson's house at Sundborn in Sweden was one of the artistic houses that revolutionised attitudes to lifestyle and domestic design at the turn of the 20th century. His watercolours of light interiors, sparsely furnished with simple painted furniture have the same characteristics as those of Gustav Stickley, MH Baillie-Scott and Charles Rennie Mackintosh. Loose rugs of striking design are strategically positioned on bare-board floors to give directional emphasis. Furniture is built in, or proportioned specifically to complement the architecture of the room – to fill the space beneath a window or to frame an intimate enclosure around the fire. The textiles, in particular, are fresh and light: they suggest a breeze about the window; bed hangings create an ethereal translucence; and the woven patterns of upholstery are strong and original in colour and texture. Every individually designed element in a room adheres to a single coherent vision of the house as a work of art. This concept of *Gesamtkunstwerke*, however, so relentlessly pursued by some architects in Europe and America – to the extent that they dictated the tone of their clients' clothes to match interiors – is more loosely structured in Larsson's work. His watercolours reveal a broader field of vision, a more eclectic sensibility to visual trends, which cast the work of his architect contemporaries in a new light.

At the turn of the 20th century, photographs and watercolours of the ideal home were more influential than the buildings that they portrayed. Architects, such as CFA Voysey, commissioned photographs of their houses before their clients could fill them with clutter and Baillie Scott's watercolours were more instrumental in the creation of his reputation than the houses he built. There is a mistaken belief, nevertheless, that these photographs and watercolours are important, primarily, as architectural records, as monuments to the ephemeral interiors that they portrayed. It was only the fact that they were conceived to encourage new commissions that this notion was allowed to persist.

The Larsson house fits with a separate set of cultural references. Carl Larsson trained as a painter rather than an architect and the house at Sundborn belongs to a Victorian fascination with the lives of artists as influential celebrities. Certainly it was an artistic house, decorated and furnished by Carl and his wife Karin with uncompromising individuality and style. It was, however, the paintings that were important and his portraits of the interiors, ostensibly begun in bad weather when the plein air series that he was working on proved impossible, reflect the concerns of artists in the 1890s rather than those of architects.

As a youthful painter in Paris, Larsson had absorbed the freshness and immediacy of plein-air painting. He understood the soft informality of Renoir's family portraits, the topicality of painting the middle classes relaxing in the sunshine on the banks of the Seine, and the dynamic insouciance of cropped compositions by Degas and Lautrec. He collected Japanese prints but he was also familiar with the sentimental charm of Kate Greenaway's illustrations. All of these stylistic influences informed the series of watercolours of his own home, which ultimately made Larsson a household name in his native Sweden. It was the role of 19th-century artists to symbolise and distil the prevailing issues of their day and Larsson's images of the home promised a reconciliation between domestic harmony and modernity. His interiors are peopled with incidental portraits of his family. Dishevelled children, artistically clad in stripy smocks make the progressive interiors seem more real, more achievable. The ideal of the happy family, the contented servant and the wife absorbed in the creative satisfactions of home-making had a profound appeal in a century of shifting social hierarchies which Larsson deployed to his advantage.

Like the watercolours of his architect contemporaries, Larsson's idealised images enjoyed an independent currency in books, magazines and exhibitions. *Ett hem*, a volume comprising 20 of his paintings, published in 1899, was the first of several immensely popular books describing his house and family. Their appeal was such that even in their own life times Carl and Karin gave day-trippers guided tours of their home; today the house is a national monument with 60,000 visitors a year. The interiors are preserved just as they appear in the paintings and yet they are not the same. After the clarity of Larsson's watercolours, and the implicit narratives suggested by his cropped compositions, the solid walls and objects that crowd in on the visitor are confusing. Grounded by reality and the specifics of time and place, the three-dimensional building lacks the emotional versatility of one of Larsson's paintings. It is a document, substantiating the content of the paintings. The art lay elsewhere, in the selective process of image-making itself, and the spaces that Larsoon created for the imagination to inhabit. ∆